# Young Man's Mischief, In the Pursuit of Happiness

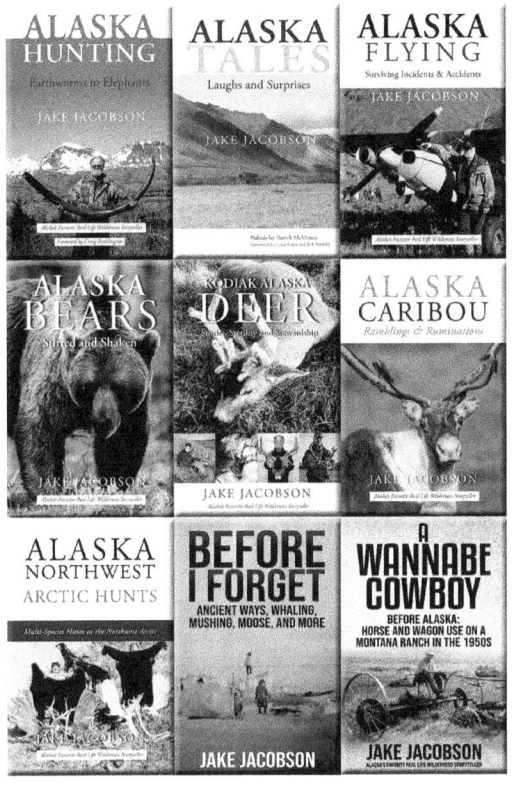

# Other Recent Books by Jake Jacobson

*ALASKA HUNTING*: Earthworms to Elephants
*ALASKA TALES*: Laughs and Surprises
*ALASKA FLYING*: Surviving Incidents and Accidents
*ALASKA BEARS*: Stirred and Shaken
*KODIAK ALASKA DEER*: Stories, Sterility and Stewardship
*ALASKA CARIBOU*: Ramblings & Ruminations
*ALASKA NW ARCTIC HUNTS:* Multi-Species Hunts in the Northwest Arctic
*BEFORE I FORGET*; Stories of Ancient Men, Whaling, Moose, Mushing and More
*WANNABE COWBOY:* Before Alaska: Horse and wagon use on a Montana ranch in the 1950s

# Young Man's Mischief, In the Pursuit of Happiness

### Jake Jacobson
Alaska's Favorite Real Life Wilderness Storyteller

*8370 Eleusis Drive, Anchorage, Alaska 99502-4630*
*books@publicationconsultants.com—www.publicationconsultants.com*

ISBN Number:978-1-63747-397-9
eBook ISBN Number: 978-1-63747-398-6

Library of Congress Number: 2024911460

Copyright © 2024 Jake Jacobson
—First Edition—

All rights reserved, including the right of reproduction in any form, or by any mechanical or electronic means including photocopying or recording, or by any information storage or retrieval system, in whole or in part in any form, and in any case not without the written permission of the author.

Manufactured in the United States of America

# INTRODUCTION

How time does fly. My debut on earth was well prior to the midpoint of the previous century. That sounds like I might be getting ... old. Naw, I prefer to believe, I'm just more experienced.

After years of toying with the idea, I decided a while back to recount some experiences and memories from my life, but the thought of an autobiography repelled me. After all, everyone has memorable tales, so why would mine be of any special interest to anyone else, anyway? But recounting specific incidences, some of which seem unique, seemed a less presumptive and maybe even, a worthwhile endeavor.

In my short time on this wonderful earth - more than three-quarters of a century, so far - four score and more years, actually - life in the United States of America and around the world has changed dramatically in more ways than I can be aware of, let alone write about. But I am familiar with some huge changes and I am uncomfortable with many of them. I'm more comfortable with the simpler life of the past, but then, probably we all revere the past because we survived it. For sure some of the changes have resulted in more comfort, security, improved - but far more expensive, health services, and better television reception with many more broadcasting stations, and remote controls, for starters. Home computers and cell phones.... wow! But the losses, outweigh the benefits as I see it. The slower, less stressful way of life was preferable to me and to most of us, I presume.

A reduced expectation of personal accountability and responsibility are the top of the social changes that I detest. My memories, often supported by films or photographs of times past, are both a source of comfort and sorrow to me. Our living quarters were not so comfortable and esthetically appealing back then as those now demanded by people on public welfare, and often demanded even more loudly by the paid bureaucratic advocates of welfare recipients. Back in the previous century most folks were satisfied and considered themselves to be both blessed and lucky with what they had, much of which they built for themselves.

My family did not have much money, yet we never considered ourselves to be poor. Self-reliance and doing for ourselves were part of our everyday life. I recall a Sears Catalog with a caption that read: "We live in deeds, not years." Members of our family stretched our dimes and dollars as far as possible. Personally, I have never been able to mentally keep up with inflation. A penny or a nickel still has value to me, and yes - I still reach down to pick up a penny lying on the ground - and call that a lucky day! Sometimes I find a dime!

In our prayers, we always remember to thank God for our wonderful blessings, as I always do. So, I'm slower to change than most folks, I guess, but I'm comfortable in this old worn, and scarred skin I'm wearing.

# EARLY MEMORIES

My parents were married on June 22, 1941. I was born on March 22, 1942 - nine months to the day after my folks' wedding. I guess that makes me a child of passion.

Just days after their wedding, my Dad, went off to World War II - first to Ireland, then to England. He fought with Patton's army in North Africa, Sicily, and Italy. I didn't see my father until I was past two years of age. In June 1944 Dad came home from fighting in Italy after the battle of Monte Casino in which his unit suffered a high percentage of casualties. He told me that my existence was a factor in his coming home. I always liked that idea. Once I got to know him, I felt so proud that I had somehow helped bring my Dad home.

I have a vague initial memory of Pop, and that is probably due to the stories that my family told of my first reaction to him. He was a stranger to me, and at first, I didn't warm up to him, or so I was told.

I do have cherished memories of Pop (I began calling him Pop when I was about twelve years old) taking me pheasant and duck hunting in Iowa at a very young age, sometimes in a pack on his back, purchased from an army surplus store. I recall him using Grandpa's old American Gun Company double-barreled twelve-gage shotgun on pheasants, waterfowl, and rabbits. I loved being included on his hunting trips and longed for the day when I could carry a gun alongside my Dad, to help provide food for our table. I recall him once coming home with the gunstock broken. He had tripped and used it to break his fall. I remember him coming home with a piece of walnut to replace the splintered stock. He had only hand tools to shape the raw piece of wood. He used wood rasps, chisels, and his pocket knife. After weeks of evenings of intricate work, he got it to fit into the metal, then he smoothed it with sandpaper. If our stuff got broken, without much ado, we set about fixing it. It was part of our way of life.

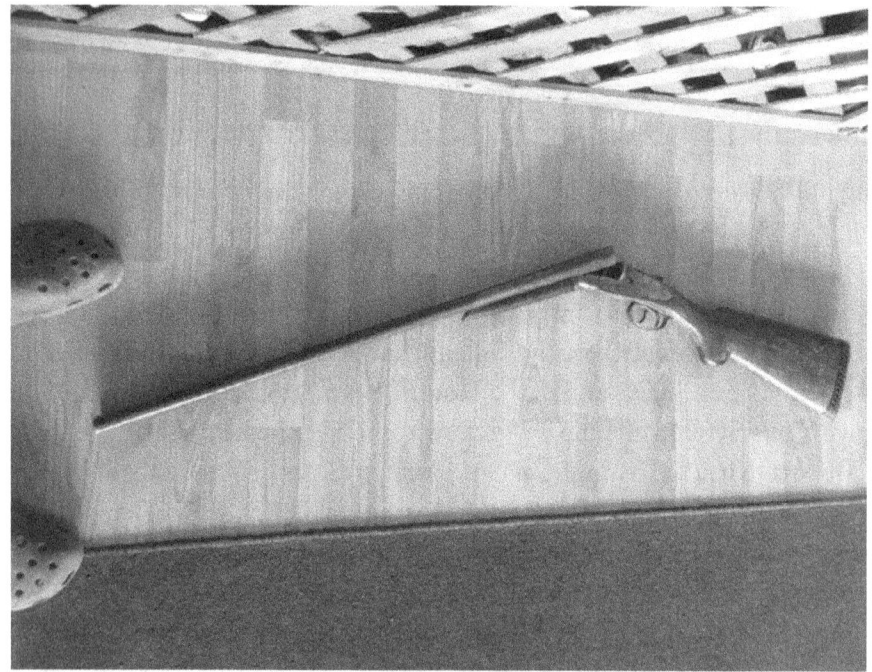

The old shotgun still in service.

Mom and Dad's families were farmers, as it seemed to my child's mind that everyone in Iowa was in those days. I had no concept of life other than being on a farm with horses, milk cows, hogs, chickens, gardens, corn fields, and outhouses. I have misty recollections of my great grandparents, the smells of home-canned fruit and vegetables, oven-baked bread, and the sometimes musty-smelling bedrooms on the second and third floors of their homes.

On my Mom's side, my great-grandpa Michael had a big stone house with large pillars made of stream-polished river rocks supporting the porch roof. His house sat near the bank of the Des Moines River and I remember seeing him and other men of the family coming and going in small boats with oars that they used to set their "trotlines" for catfish. Sometimes they brought in large carp or suckers, which we ate as well. In the living room of the big house was a huge fireplace made of river rocks similar to those of the outside pillars. On the walls hung some Indian things, such as stone axes and other primitive tools. On one side were some long black hairy pieces that we kids were told were scalps of Indians taken by our ancestors about a hundred years before.

My cousins and I had wonderful times wherever we were, but especially at the grandparents' and great-grandparents' homes. We all were treated very special and we knew we were deeply loved and valued.

In the winter of 1947, I had to get my tonsils and adenoids removed. I still remember the awful dream I had. The dream was caused by the ether anesthetic, but I also remember the nearly constant ice cream that I was fed during recovery. Ice cream indulgence notwithstanding, I sure didn't want to have to endure any more ether or throat-cutting.

## WE MOVED OFF THE FARM

Sometime after my tonsils were removed we moved to a big town, called Ottumwa, where Dad found a job in a meat packing plant. Our house was on a paved street where there were no cows, horses, or other animals. I didn't like that place, primarily due to the lack of animals and too many people that I didn't know. Wintertime was especially dreary and I missed the sounds and smells of farm animals.

Both of my Grandmas had always told me that the devil lived in the worst place imaginable, so I figured he must reside in the bottom of that dark, smelly hole in the outhouse. Shortly after moving to town, I was introduced to an inside bathroom with a flush toilet. When I heard the toilet gurgling as it flushed, I ran away in fear that the devil was struggling to get out of the mess he was in, to come up and grab me, so he could drag me down with him! It took me a long time to be at ease in any indoor bathroom. I recall that being in such close proximity to the ultimate evil one led me to try to improve my behavior, as well. I felt much more comfortable using the tried and true outhouses than indoor bathrooms. Some people spend a lot of time on the toilet seat, but I never have. For me, it's always been a quick job and out the door - and that's not due only to the frigidity of the outside air.

During the war, Grandpa Jacobson was working in a munitions plant and was injured in an explosion. The doctors told him he should move to a milder climate. Grandpa's younger brother, named Harper, worked as a barber in El Campo, Texas. Grandpa sold the small farm and the little gas station he operated for extra income, then moved the family to Texas. Soon his experience and interest in farming led him to become a rice buyer for large companies.

Soon after arriving in their new home, I noticed that some of my Texas relatives were speaking southern-accented lingo - y'all know what I mean?

But Mom's family remained on the farm in Iowa. After returning from the war my Dad worked in a meat packing plant and delivered ice before deciding to go to college on the G.I. bill. He decided that he wanted to become a mining engineer.

## The Family Heads West

In the late summer of 1947, our family, now numbering four since my sister, Pat, was born that June, pulled up stakes and set out for the great Southwest. I recall us driving to New Mexico in an old four-door Ford sedan which broke down often. Pop did the repairs himself, usually, alongside the road as Mom, my newborn sister and I stayed close by. Flat tires were almost an everyday affair and I remember Dad debating whether or not to replace a bad tire with a "retread". To stretch his meager cash on hand, a retread was purchased, but it came apart after only a few miles, so from then on, no re-treads were bought to replace ruined tires, but he often purchased used tires.

Mom kept busy on our migratory trip with sewing or knitting and minding us kids as Dad frequently had to work on the aged Ford. Everything we owned was in that old sedan.

When we drove into Socorro, New Mexico, Mom expressed her dismay at the desolate countryside and I thought that place was really not very nice. That rocky, dry, creosote bush-covered country along the Rio Grande River was a far cry from the green, fertile, rolling hills of Iowa. But Dad reminded us all that we only had to be there for four years and once that time had passed, we would all have a better life. Only four years? That was most of my life!

"M" Mountain near Socorro. Creosote or "Greasewood" was the dominant flora.

At first, we lived in a small Shultz trailer. I remember Dad and some of his friends hard at studying way past my bedtime at the small kitchen table. I recall them all speaking of how difficult Quantitative Analysis, or "Quant" was. When I got to college, I soon learned first-hand just how tough that subject was.

Cigarette smoking was common back then. Both my parents smoked, but to save money, they rolled their own with a little hand-cranked machine. Littering was common too, resulting in lots of cigarette and some cigar butts lying about wherever people walked. As a preschool kid, I picked up some discarded cigarette butts and Mom caught me trying to smoke them. She was horrified and brought me in to tell Dad what I had been doing. One of Dad's classmates, Hugh, was present. He pulled a fresh cigar out of his pocket and suggested that if I wanted to smoke, I may as well do it right. I thought this guy was really nice as I happily drew deeply on the Roi-Tan Blunt when he held a match to it. Mom seemed to disapprove, but Dad went along with the program. The package said it was "the cigar that breaths", but in a few minutes I wished I had never breathed any of its vapors. I tried to bravely finish the nasty thing, as the adults feigned disinterest, but after a few minutes, my facial contortions and color were such that Dad picked me up and held me over the sink to vomit. The lesson was effective as I never again picked up any butts, nor did I harbor any desire to smoke until more than a decade later when I once again tried cigars. As a teenager, I figured I should give it a go again, because, after all, Grandpa Jacobson smoked cigars. But I didn't like the taste it left in my mouth, even after brushing my teeth.

I distinctly remember going to the New Mexico School of Mines initiation which was held in the school's basketball gym. Each freshman student was taken before the crowd, told to bend over and clasp their ankles, whereupon a senior student gave them some whacks - three hard ones, as I recall - with a large wooden paddle. Following that physical abuse, each freshman walked over and kissed the "Blarney Stone". I did not like it when my Dad took his turn bending over and receiving the whacks. The next day when Dad lowered his pants to check out his backside, he was badly bruised. I remember crying for him. I never could figure out the sense of such a hurtful, senseless rite of initiation.

Christmas that year, 1947, was really special. At age five, I got my first gun, a Daisy lever action BB gun, some new home-knit wool socks, and a few other little things, but it was the BB gun that made my day! That same morning as the turkey roasted in the oven, I went out and, after a number of missed shots, I finally shot two sparrows off the fence wire and brought them in for all to share in my moment of glory. My mother told me to pluck and clean them. I wound up skinning them. When I handed her the little birds, she put them in with the turkey, and, to me, they tasted just like turkey - maybe even better! My parents told me that I had better be prepared to eat anything I killed. So, my food-hunting pursuits started off deliciously - and just right.

## 1948 End of Dad's first college year in New Mexico - off to Grandpa's

Having made it through the first year, Dad got a job working for the Soil Conservation Service, surveying land, along with other projects. My Dad was a natural musician and played the clarinet, saxophone, and bass fiddle very well. He and several other students started a small band and made a little money on weekends and holidays playing for dances and other festivities. Sometimes he traveled to other towns, like Carrizozo, New Mexico, for that sort of work. It was a source of income and he needed all the financial gain he could earn, Mom got a job waiting tables at a restaurant in town, which was within walking distance from the campus. Two other couples had a daughter about my sister's age, so they "kid pooled" to avoid having to pay for a babysitter.

I really lucked out and was sent to spend the summer of 1948 with Grandpa and Grandma Jacobson in El Campo, Texas. We all drove to Fort Stockton - about midway between Socorro and El Campo - where we met Grandpa and Grandma - Grant and Minnie Jacobson. After one night in a motel with a swimming pool (the first I had ever seen), I went east and Mom and Dad headed back to Socorro.

That summer was absolutely delightful. I rode along with Grandpa when he sampled rice, I learned to play dominoes with him and the other men in his office and got treated to ice cream often. I played canasta with him, Grandma, and my Aunts, Hazel and Maysel. I was very indulged. I helped Grandma in the garden and learned how to kill, pluck, and singe chickens. I liked the idea of chopping the chickens' heads off with a small ax, but Grandma would lay the chicken on the ground, place a broomstick over the neck step on the broomstick and just pull the chicken loose from its head, tossing the body away so its wild flopping would not get so much blood on her shoes and clothes. Also, she figured it was safer for me to kill them by that method, rather than by using an ax with which I might lop off a finger or two of my own.

Grandpa and Grandma's house in El Campo, Texas

Grandma made a chicken and rice goulash that I preferred, even over her wonderful pies and other desserts. I've never, to this day, been able to discover her recipe or anything that tastes so good.

Every Sunday we attended the Methodist Church and three mornings each week I spent in Vacation Bible School. I was always kept busy with interesting things. It seemed that everything was fun. Life was wonderful!

And we went fishing a lot. Some of the rice farmers had ponds stocked with largemouth bass and bluegills which they were happy to have me tempt with my cane pole and a red worm bait while Grandpa checked their rice and storage facilities. Adults warned me to be extra careful around the water as Cottonmouth Water Moccasins were common in the area, so I stayed away from all snakes and was careful where I put my hands and feet. So, it was caution - but not paralysis - regarding snakes for me. Earthworms were the most effective bait and the little cork made it easy for me to know when to set the hook. When Grandpa had to spend time with the farmers, I was more than happy to spend time with their fish. Grandpa kept a small ice box in the car to keep my catches cold. Grandma always praised me for bringing home fresh fish. Fried, the little bluegills and perch tasted best, but the largemouth bass were my favorite to catch.

I remember the excitement and amazement of everyone, especially myself when I caught a five-pound bass on a little perch hook that had only a tiny piece of worm on it. It was my biggest fish, so far.

Frequently we went fishing in salt water, either in the inter-coastal canal or in one of the bays. I preferred saltwater fishing as one never knew what type of fish he might catch. Small saltwater catfish were considered a nuisance and not kept for eating - their dried carcasses littered the shore, but they were numerous and kept us busy, while the larger "gaff top" catfish was a tasty keeper. We caught croakers, redfish, speckled trout (spotted weakfish), drum, and many other species. On rare occasions, someone would hook a small shark, which was exciting! At night we sometimes gigged

flounders, being ever cautious to avoid sting rays. Grandpa did the gigging while I watched from shore.

Grandpa had a small casting net with which he usually caught all the bait we needed, but if wild bait wasn't available, shrimp could be purchased inexpensively almost anywhere. Even the gas stations had shrimp - in live, frozen, or refrigerated form to sell for bait.

Most of the gas stations had the old-style pump that required someone to use a lever to fill a glass cylinder with fuel, then use the nozzle to transfer it into the vehicle.

Blue crabs were numerous in some bays and Grandma specialized in catching them. She put a piece of bait (usually a fish head or carcass after the fillets were removed) on a string, then when she felt something tugging at the bait, she would carefully raise the string and scoop up the crabs using a hand-held dip net. I learned early on that those crustaceans were fast and accurate with their claws after I got pinched a time or two. The activities all came together to make our fishing trips great fun.

Grandma was often worried that, when fishing, I did not eat nearly enough - such was my concentration. I sure wanted to grow larger, but I figured that fishing was not apt to stunt my growth as I could always catch up with sandwiches and cookies on the way home, and, as Grandpa told me, I could only catch a fish if I had bait in the water and was paying attention. We mostly fished with bait and corks (or bobbers), but sometimes we fished with a sinker on the bottom, which required closer concentration. I loved it all.

At my Grandparents' house, as at home, I put my "play clothes" on for fishing and play, but kept my newer, better, duds for church and other social occasions ... including school. Now, more than seven decades later, I still use my "play clothes" for most activities and am most comfortable in them. Old habits are hard to break, which in some cases is a good thing.

Among my memories is a temporarily terrifying afternoon when several neighborhood kids and I were playing a combat game. For some reason, I was not accompanying Grandpa that afternoon. In our fantasy, we Romans were battling some pagan hoard. We were using garbage can lids as shields and sticks for swords. One of the new boys picked up a pitchfork and hurled it at his opponent, as the "bad guy" fled. One of the tines of the hay fork pierced the boy's calf, knocking him to the ground. All the kids, especially the boy with the spear in his leg, panicked and began yelling and crying. I ran the half block or so to Grandma's house and told her what happened. She stopped what she was doing and ran with me to the scene. When she saw the screaming, speared kid, she told others to run home and tell their parents. The mother of the speared kid arrived and was pretty calm. She told the boy to stop crying as she pulled the spear out. Only one of the tines had pierced his leg. I still have a mental image of the red blood oozing from the small round wound. That incident ended our epic Roman battles ... at least for a while. I went to visit the speared boy that evening. His Mom had dosed it liberally with Merthiolate, which we called "Devil's spit", and wrapped a large section of white cloth she had torn from a clean sheet around his leg. That evening he was grinning as he scooped up large spoons full of ice cream and offered me a bowlful, which I happily accepted. The next day the boy was playing softball with us, proudly wearing the large bandage. He was a hero in his own mind and in the minds of some of the other kids. I admired his courage and the fact that he was playing hard the next day.

    Grandpa and Grandma gave me a long discussion about how common sense should always prevail in all our activities and how awful things could turn out if we didn't use our heads. I was sure glad that I had not been the one to cast the spear ... or to get pinioned by the pitchfork javelin. And I was glad it hit his leg and not his belly.

    Another afternoon I walked over to my great uncle Harper's home to play with some of my second cousins who lived at the edge of town. It seemed that everything grew well and quickly in that humid, sunny area of southeast Texas. The drainage ditches on either side of the road were choked with tall grass and weeds. Some younger kids were playing in the ditches, wading in and out of the water. One little girl suddenly let forth a hysterical scream and a nearby kid yelled "snake!" Kids fled the ditches like popcorn vacating a frying pan. Adults materialized from all quarters. One older man with a shovel hollered "Mocassin" and began stabbing at the weeds with his shovel. He tossed a large, thick, ugly black snake up onto the road and chopped the head off. Another man took the little girl, bitten on her lower leg, to the doctor.

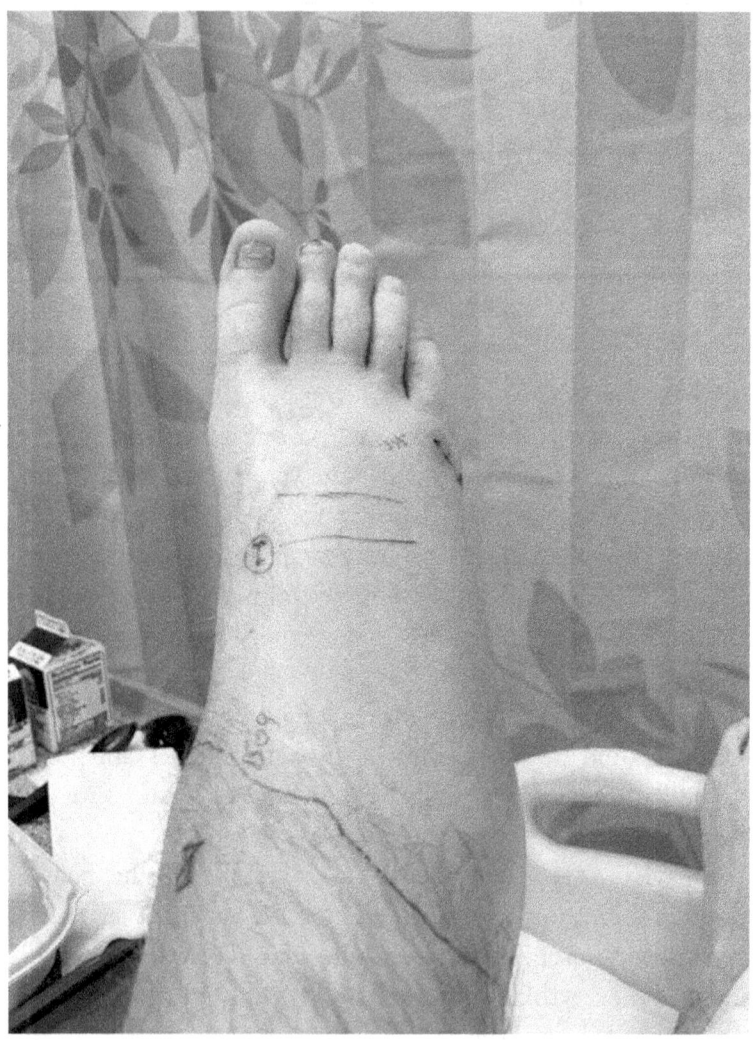

A neighbor teenage boy got bit near the ankle by a moccasin.

My uncle Grant taught in the Aggie school and knew plenty about animals, including snakes. He came over later that afternoon to tell me that the cottonmouth (*Agkistrodon piscivorus*) was a very aggressive and dangerous serpent. There were Copperheads and Rattlesnakes in the area, too. He spent the evening telling me how dangerous and bad most snakes are and that we kids should stay away from all snakes. But it was chicken goulash night and the spooky stories did not deter my appetite. However, I always gave the ditches a wide berth after that.

A week or so later, Uncle Grant took me to visit the little girl, whose parents wanted all the kids to see how bad snakes and their bites could be. Her leg was still very swollen and discolored with a blue and purplish appearance, but her mother said she was getting better. I decided that I wanted nothing to do with snakes. Spiders, except for Daddy Long Legs, were on my avoidance list, too.

Time seems to last longer for kids - I've noticed this as I've gotten older, but all too soon, it was time for me to go back to New Mexico. I never liked Socorro, and especially after the first summer in El Campo, the dry creosote bush country of Socorro would never look good to me. I figured that is why the nicest country is always the most crowded.

## BACK TO NEW MEXICO AND INTO SCHOOL - FALL, 1948

Before school resumed my grandparents drove me back home. Dad had been offered an opportunity to rent a small two-bedroom apartment on the campus which was a real improvement over the tiny trailer.

My first day of school in August 1948, was long anticipated and most welcomed by me. My Dad was going to school and now, so was I - just like my Dad. I was one proud six-year-old boy.

The ethnic demographics of Socorro showed a predominance of Hispanic people - Mexicans. Many of the school teachers were of that culture and spoke with a very strong Mexican accent. Like the other kids from the Midwest, I soon was talking with a Hispanic accent without even realizing it. My first teacher, Mrs. Baca, put several of us into her "advanced" group which she called the "Beesabees". None of us knew just what that meant, but we got to do more things than most of the other kids and we were her favorites, so any name was fine with us.

At the Christmas program, my Mom asked Mrs. Baca what "Beesabees" meant. After some time-consuming, heavily accented, and frustrating explanation, we came to understand that our group was actually named the "Busy Bees".

The student housing area where we rented was on the edge of the college campus, separated by a dirt road and a three-wire, barbed wire fence from the dry, creosote bush and tumbleweed-choked, desert. A local rancher kept a few cows and calves in the area and we kids were told to not cross the fence, but of course, we did. The range cattle paid us little attention and we kept an eye out for a bull but never saw one. We'd see cottontail rabbits frequently and occasionally a large jackrabbit. We used our bow and arrows to try to take rabbits and our BB guns for lizards and insects from grasshoppers to vinegaroons. The nasty-looking Vinegaroons, or whip tailed scorpions, would spray out a liquid that smelled like vinegar, but in spite of their horrid appearance, were harmless. We usually either killed or ignored the occasional Vinegaroon we happened upon. I wondered why God created vinegaroons and hornets.

A Vinegaroo

One afternoon I saw a strange-looking flat lizard with spikes around the back of its head. This was a life form entirely new to me. I found it out in the open and discovered that it was not nearly as fast as most lizards. It was fierce-looking, but I decided to catch it. When I had it cornered and reached to grab it, the feisty-looking little beast squirted blood on me - and, most horrifying of all - the blood came from its eye! Astounded and confused, I withdrew my hand, let that spooky miniature dinosaur go its own way, and I headed for home. That evening one of Dad's friends said it must have been a "Horny Toad" and it spit blood at me because I scared it, but he added that those strange little

Our pet "Horned Toad."

critters were harmless. Not long after that, I found another Horned Toad and picked it up by its "horns". This one didn't spit on me and I kept it for two weeks in a large clear glass jar, with Mom's permission. I had seen the Horney Toad on a large anthill, slurping up ants as fast as it could, so I caught ants off the same anthill by holding a piece of dry grass near the main hole. When ants began climbing up the grass stalk, I put the stalk with clinging ants in a large glass jar. They couldn't scale the smooth sides to get out. After I had a couple of dozen grass pieces in the jar, I would cap it and take it home for the lizard. It was great evening entertainment for the whole family to watch our new lizard friend gobble up the ants that I had gathered to release in its box. It seemed he could consume as many ants as I gave him. If I stroked its back, the little fellow would turn one side down and the other side up.

He (we didn't know but what it could have been a "her") seemed to like the attention. It was a very personable short-term pet. After two weeks, I took "Horny" back to his favorite ant hill and said goodbye. Dad said that similar critters lived in Australia and Africa. I wanted to visit both of those wild-sounding places.

The Rio Grande River ran south toward Mexico and was only a short distance east of downtown Socorro. We sometimes took wieners for a picnic along the sandy banks of the river. Mom found wild asparagus and picked quite a lot the first time we were there. Cooked with butter and garlic, it was delicious. Mom said we were living off the land. I liked the sound of that. That gave us reason enough to return.

Dad bought two metal telescoping fishing poles for six dollars each, and knowing how much I loved to fish, he took me fishing every chance he got (of course he liked fishing, too). We caught largemouth bass and catfish mostly and we soon learned that catfishing was better at night. I liked the night fishing with a small lantern nearby, the owls hooting, and other night sounds. But in warm conditions the mosquitoes were bothersome. We used a little glass jar of insect repellant that Dad bought at the Army surplus store for a dime. It didn't smell nice, but the bugs seemed to dislike it more than we did. And it did help keep the pestiferous insects off us.

Then Dad took up hand fishing during warm weather. He would get in the water with just his shorts on and grope around in the water underneath the banks and brush to grab live catfish. He caught bigger catfish that way than we ever did by using a hook and line, but I was spooked that the spines would pierce me. I'd had a couple of punctures from barbs of small catfish and knew how painful they can become and how slow they were to heal. Mom said she absolutely did not want me to do any hand fishing. She was thinking of snakes. At age six, I didn't argue on that issue.

Sometimes on weekends, we would drive north to the Indian pueblos to trade clothes, comic books, toys, magazines, food, and almost anything else we had that might interest the Indians. It was sort of a swap meet situation. The friendly Indians had pottery and jewelry made of silver inlaid with turquoise. Most often we went to the Isleta Pueblo around twelve miles south of Albuquerque and then on to the Sandia Pueblo which sat about eight miles north of Albuquerque, which was the biggest town in the state. It seemed like a long trip and I was always filled with anticipation of what treasures we might find. Trading with the Indians was great fun. I looked upon each trip as a sort of adventure. I wished I could have been there to deal with the Indians a hundred years earlier. Kit Carson was already a hero of mine.

**Our special treat on road trips.**

A highlight of going to Albuquerque was stopping to get a LottaBurger - "A Square Meal on a Round Bun" the signs said. Those were the best-tasting hamburgers I ever encountered - and, they were belly stuffing big!

Even at a young age, I was surprised that so many people would decide to live the primitive lifestyle that the Indians chose. Most of all, I was amazed that they lived clustered in such a crowded place. I would certainly have been living out in the wildest corners of their reservation, but most people of all cultures like to be close to others, I guess. Not me, though.

Socorro grade school had no Indian students, or at least we weren't aware of any. Mexicans (now referred to as Hispanics or Mexican-Americans) made up most of the student population, with Caucasian kids being about thirty percent or less of the student body. I recollect that everyone seemed to accept everybody else. I began to pick up words in the Spanish language and I sometimes seemed to have a Spanish accent.

On Saturdays, we often got to go to the movies, downtown. It cost seventeen cents admission and Big Hunk candy bars were two for a nickel. Serial movie episode stories - to be continued - were common and we kids longed for the next segment.

One of the downtown bars, where Hugh liked to drink beer.

The movie theater was near the town square, which had several saloons. One of my Dad's classmates, Hugh, often spent his Saturday nights in one of the bars and would drink an entire case of beer - twenty-four bottles in one evening. I was amazed. My Dad told me that his friend Hugh's special "ability" was nothing for anyone to be proud of.

During my first grade year, I became suddenly aware of and interested in the anatomical differences between boys and girls. Of course, doctors knew all about that kind of stuff, so it seemed reasonable that we should play "the doctor game" at any opportunity that was at least semi-private. I'd been working on increasing my knowledge of female anatomy with a neighbor girl when news of my investigations reached my parents. Mom and Dad were not pleased and told me that game was on the forbidden list. To make their point crystal clear, I was to get a whipping. As part of my punishment, I was to select an appropriate switch and present it to my Dad.

That was an effective bit of child psychology my folks used on me. I went out to look for a switch, dreading its eventual application on my derriere in my punishment. Finally, I found a limp piece of large rope and tested it on my leg. It wasn't at all intolerable, so I took that to Dad. When he saw my selection, he tossed it aside, bent me over his knee, and used his open hand. He laid to the task with vigor to the point that I thought I might never be able to breathe again. The "doctor game" was deleted from my repertoire of possible games to play with neighbor girls - at least for a time. I would resign myself to have to continue to live in relative ignorance.

## END OF FIRST GRADE

The next summer, **1949,** my parents took me to Fort Stockton again to meet Grandpa and Grandma Jacobson. I went home with them to the wonderful, fertile place they lived in South East Texas - El Campo …. and to the fishing, garden chores, chicken killing and plucking, as well as Vacation Bible School. I was looking forward to resuming all of those activities.

That summer Grandma got a big surprise. She had long wanted a "deep freeze" and Grandpa bought a new one for her. (I doubt there were any used ones available.) When we came home with more fish than we could eat at a big meal, Grandma would prepare the fish, place them in an empty waxed milk carton (another new item), fill it with clean water, and freeze it into a block. The fish kept very well and tasted to me, at my seven years of age, like they were freshly caught when she thawed the carton out and cooked the fish.

We did some longer fishing trips that summer, we went all the way to Aransas Pass and Corpus Christi one weekend, and of course, we fished along the way every chance we got. We saw one man catch and land a Tarpon - it was a huge fish, but people said they were not good to eat. One beach held the rotting carcass of an Alligator Gar. I was impressed by its jaws and teeth and wanted to bring the head home, but Grandma said it was way too stinky, so it stayed on the beach, neglected, to my great dismay. I was more than ready to tolerate the smell if I could keep those fierce-looking jaws and teeth. So began a fascination with mega-fauna and teeth that has never left me.

I recall evenings during rainy or windy weather, sitting at the large dining room table snapping peas or cracking and picking pecans. The constant loving banter and teasing made fun of what otherwise might have seemed tedious chores.

I remember going with my Uncle Grant to castrate some little pigs. I helped hold their legs as he did the surgery. The poor little porkers' struggles and squeals bothered me a lot, but Grant explained to me that we had to do it so the pigs would grow faster, fight less with each other, and taste better when it became time to eat them. He told me that without a useful purpose, those pigs wouldn't even exist. I guessed that sort of life was better than no life at all ... and I did like to eat pork. I figured the same must apply to the ferocious bulls that the matadors killed in the bullfights, as being mean and aggressive was their sole purpose in life.

## BACK TO NEW MEXICO VIA COLORADO

I awoke one morning to the realization that the summer was almost gone again and I had to go back to Socorro, but Grandpa thought we should take a look at parts of Colorado on the way. We drove North to Dallas, then on to Amarillo, and up to Denver. The country turned from the lush green of Southeast Texas to the over-cooked Texas panhandle, which then got steadily nicer as we approached the Front Range and Denver. We didn't spend much time in any one place, we just drove through to see the country. The Rocky Mountains seemed better than the flat, dry plains, but those big, steep, densely wooded, mountains were not appealing to me. I preferred a country that one could walk around in and see more of, without so much effort. After about a week of car travel, along with reciting rhymes and singing (Grandpa would sing a little tune "Oh, it's fourteen miles from Whippleton to Whappleton," and I never did find out where either place was), we arrived at my parents place - home - which looked pretty good to me.

Two of Dad's classmates spent a lot of time in our kitchen, devouring Mom's wonderful pies as they studied. To me, it seemed they always talked about Alaska, where one had been a trapper at Manley Hot Springs and the other was an Indian from a village in the same area. Without even trying, those men convinced me that I just had to see Alaska. I was pretty sure that if fishing, hunting, and trapping were even close to as good as they told me, I would become a full-time Alaskan.

That school year, second grade, went along pretty well and I was given a used bicycle which expanded my range of adventures. I could peddle pretty quickly over to the home of my best friend, Jeepers Funk, and from there we two boys did what most young fellows do. We got into minor trouble from time to time, but nothing serious. We mostly just had innocent fun and played a few little pranks. We saw where kids had vandalized things, but we were angered by such activities.

The old school desks were made so that the lift-top table on one desk had a fold-down bench on the front. I sat on the bench of the desk behind me and the kid in front used the bench from my desk. Lined up properly they made efficient seating for school kids. Those desktops had a hole for an ink bottle - inkwells, they were called. Ballpoint pens weren't in common use yet. It was tempting, beyond my ability to resist, to dip the tip of the braided hair of the unfortunate girl in front into my ink bottle. That brought me a reprimand - a swat or two in front of the class -every time I did it.

The grade school desks were very efficient.

Placing lizards, frogs, toads, or bugs inside the desks, especially that of the teacher, who reacted more dramatically than the girls in the class, also got me some swats.

The teacher would have the kid about to be punished come to the front of the class, bend over, and grasp his ankles. I don't recall a girl ever getting swatted. The paddle was built a bit like a canoe paddle, but smaller. Three stinging smacks of the paddle did a lot of good in helping us remember what was forbidden. But everyone is entitled to some fun and some of the boys, like Jeepers and me, needed frequent reminders of what not to do. We kept finding new no-nos. If I got a swat at school I was to tell my Dad and Mom and would receive at least as many swats from them. If I did not 'fess up, my swats were doubled, if and when the folks found out. I seldom risked not telling my parents about school discipline issues.

But we weren't mean, bad kids. Vandalism was never our thing. Our pranks were pretty normal, I think.

One fine spring day I found a small pond that was just brimming with tadpoles. Having never seen one before, I was fascinated. I located a discarded jar with a lid nearby, so I put a few of the squirming taddies in the jar with water and took them home. My Dad told me that in a while they would grow legs, then turn into little frogs, but I should take them back to where I found them. I figured watching those body changes in the little creatures would be really amazing. Unbeknownst to my parents, on Friday of that week - which was show and tell day - I took a small jar with about a dozen tadpoles puttering around in its water to school to show the other kids. I selected nice big, fat tadpoles. I secreted the jar in my desk, for maximum surprise and effect when I showed it to the class. I was pretty sure that my presentation would earn me some sort of praise, due to the amazing nature of my discovery. I put small air holes in the lid, so my captives could breathe.

But, alas, the show and tell session that day got canceled because the principal found some other event for us, and I forgot to take my tadpoles out of my desk drawer. I remembered the taddies on Saturday when I went to the movie, but had no way of rescuing them. I figured they would probably be okay. When I told Jeepers about my taddies, he agreed that they would surely be all right.

(I would like to make contact with Jeepers Funk, if anyone has any contact information on him, please contact me.)

But, no, when I entered the school building on Monday morning, a nauseating stench pervaded the entire area and was strongest in my homeroom. I remembered my tadpoles, but they had never before smelled like that! Upon entering the room, two girls vomited and the teacher called in the janitor. All the kids were acting sick and some were bent over and hollering for "Ralph", or maybe it was for "Europe" - and we weren't even studying geography.

As I sat down at my desk, the awful truth dawned on me. I opened the desk lid to peek inside and nearly got sick myself. My tadpoles had morphed into a sickening-looking slimy grey jelly that was emitting that horrible smell through the little holes I had punched in the lid of the jar so they could breathe - and stay alive.

That uniquely nauseating odor never left my memory - or membrain? I never experienced it again until twelve years later when I got into a row with a fat fellow at the local swimming pool where I was one of two lifeguards. The sweaty obese kid got a hammerlock on my head and my nose wound up close to one of his armpits. I blurted out that he smelled like putrified tadpoles, to which he and the kids watching the battle, all began laughing, and the fight ended.

The teacher, Mrs. Salazar zeroed in on me and found the jar. She struggled to keep from throwing up (she was making urping sounds and her belly was convulsing - it sounded like she too, was saying "Europe", or maybe it was Ralph,) as she seized my arm and marched me quick step, jar in hand, to the principal's office. As we entered his large office, the principal immediately placed one hand over his nose and asked the teacher what that awful smell was.

"I theenk Meester Jacobson here, (she had to pause as she convulsed) should tell you why the school steenks so bad," said Mrs. Salazar.

Feeling worse for the poor helpless little tadpoles than for my perilous situation, I told the principal it was me who caused the stink. I also explained that the little critters were for show and tell on Friday, but he had canceled the program and I just forgot about my little frog taddies until Saturday, but that was too late to save them. Besides, my friend and I thought they would be fine for the weekend with the air holes in the lid.

The Principal, Mr. Torres, by then ready to up-chuck himself, told me to take the jar outside right away and wait for the janitor.

I headed for the swing set and put the jar on the ground. I was enjoying a leisurely swing when the janitor arrived. He was wearing a handkerchief over his face - kind of like an old-time bandit or highwayman. He told me to pick up the jar and follow him to a large garbage can, which is where the jellied tadpoles ended up.

As we walked back toward the door, kids were pouring out into the fresh air. Several teachers accompanied the kids and told everyone that we would have recess early that day. The teachers looked especially miserable. I was sure I heard people calling for "Ralph". Somehow the smell lingered in the building - and our memories - long after the tadpoles' departure.

Jeepers and I talked about the debacle and decided that tadpoles just don't make good pets.

Most of us boys took our marbles out of our pockets and began some games. The girls played hopscotch or jacks. I believe I won five or six marbles that morning, including two cat-eyes, which was much better than average for me.

Some parents came to school to pick up their sick kids, but most of us had to resume classes just after lunchtime. The school smelled like Clorox and Pine-Sol when we went back inside.

It's amazing to me yet, that the odor was so pervasive, and memorable, without the jar even being spilled.

My friend Jeepers told all the other kids about me and my tadpoles. Soon I gained the status of temporary minor hero with my schoolmates. My rise to glory came accidentally, but I enjoyed my brief moment of fame.

I was never punished for that incident, as I guess Mr. Salazar felt a twinge of responsibility for canceling the show-and-tell program.

The school was great fun and I got to be a crossing guard while still just in second grade. I was issued a plastic helmet liner from a real World War II helmet and a white canvas slash to wear. The helmet was so big, I looked absolutely ridiculous, but I felt pretty important and protective of the younger kids. Some of the older boys razed me a little, but I figured they were jealous, and, so I just concentrated on doing my job.

My skill at playing marbles was never the best, but I was cautious and sometimes wound up ahead. Then sometime later came the tops that all the boys carried in their pockets. We played games before school, during recess, lunch, and after school if situations permitted. Sometimes hard candy was wagered in the top spinning games. I avoided playing with kids who used unwrapped hard candy, some of which looked like it had been stored in their dirty pockets, or coated with axle grease.

Whether through winning or otherwise winding up with some clean candy, I would always take it home to split fifty-fifty with my little sister, Pat.

Each top came with a string to get it spinning.

Tops came into vogue, big time. We had little wooden tops, some had rounded ends and some had spikes. The tops cost a nickel apiece, whether they had sharp or rounded points. A person could do more tricks with the rounded ones, sometimes picking the spinning top up in the palm of the hand. A game evolved whereby one kid would throw his top and with it spinning, another boy would try to throw his right on top of the spinning one, trying to split it. Some of the boys sharpened the spikes on their tops to make splitting others easier. I never thought much of that destructive game. I wanted my tops to last, after all, they cost a whole nickel each.

We took our lunch to school in a little metal container called a "lunch bucket." New from the store, they came with a small thermos bottle that fit in the lid, but the thermos bottles had glass liners which were soon broken. I didn't miss mine, as I usually drank water anyway and that was available free from a fountain at school. Mom routinely planned to make more supper than we would eat and used the leftovers for Dad's lunch and mine. I often ate meatloaf sandwiches, eggplant sandwiches, spaghetti sandwiches ... whatever. As I figured it, anything beat an air sandwich. I was never a picky eater. I never heard of a School Hot Lunch Program until I was in seventh grade.

A typical lunch box.

Yo-yos made their appearance on the school scene. There were the standard ones and the "sleepers".

I remember my Mother saving her tips and other bits of change in a Mason jar. After what seemed like half of forever to me - and it no doubt seemed much longer for her - when she finally had saved enough money to buy a used wringer washing machine, Dad took us all to an appliance store and Mom picked her washer from several used machines. The thing stood on four legs and had a round belly tub with a black agitator inside that swished the clothes and water back and forth when she plugged it into an electrical socket. After the wash, the water was drained and replaced with clean water for the rinse. When the rinse was completed, Mom would turn the wringer crank handle. The two rollers would engage the clothes that were fed through and squeeze the water from them. One had to be careful to not feed fingers into the rollers. The water drained back into the tub. The clothes were placed into a basket and taken outside to hang up to dry. This saved so much time over washing the clothes by hand in the kitchen sink or a galvanized tub with a washboard and then squeezing the water out by twisting. She was so proud of her washing machine. I think it cost about seventeen dollars. ( I calculated that was a hundred trips to the Saturday matinee movies.) She normally did the washing on Saturday and I remember her saying how quick and easy it had become.

Mom's machine looked like this but ours had a crank handle to turn the rollers.

Mom repeatedly reminded us all that one had to be careful to not adjust the rollers too close to each other, or buttons would be broken. Zippers were not in common use in the 1940s. Velcro wasn't even a dream yet.

I usually got the job of hanging up the clothes and bringing them and the clothespins in when everything was dry. By standing on a milk crate or a blasting powder box I could just reach the lines to place the clothes pins. I remember when the new type of clothespins with metal springs came out. Before that, we had all wooden pins that were cut to size. One had to be careful to not jam them too hard onto a piece of laundry, bacause the one-piece wooden pins were easily split.

A new invention came out that Mom wanted to try. It was an expanding wireframe. The metal frame could be fit down into each pant leg. Once in place, it could be spread out to give the pants an ironed look when they dried. It was a time saver for most ladies of that era who ironed pants. I thought those wireframes might be useful for drying animal skins, but the animals I was getting were dwarfed by the pants frames. I did find some stiff wire that I bent to work okay for drying cottontail rabbits, ground squirrels, and such.

We had a small radio and listened to the news in the evening, but Dad usually had to skip that due to the demands of his school study and work. It seemed he was forever having to use any spare time he had to work on the old Ford to keep it running.

One night in the fall of 1949 Dad came home after dark, covered with blood. When I saw him, I began to cry. It looked to me like he had been shot. He gathered me up, hugged me, and laughed, then took me outside to see what he had in the trunk of the car. He had killed a big mule deer buck with Grandpa's old twelve-gage shotgun while hunting up near the little town of Magdalena. I thought the deer was beautiful, even though one antler was badly misshapen.

Mom and Dad worked late into the night preparing the meat and when we got the first taste the next day, I told them that I liked it almost as much as Grandma Jacobson's chicken goulash.

The following spring Dad and his two Alaskan classmates, Bill and Walt decided they would go prospecting for several days in search of silver. As things developed, with Mom working, it would be less inconvenient for everyone if I went with the men. So began my first big wilderness adventure.

We packed picks and shovels and camping gear back into some pretty desolate mountains using horses and a couple of burros. We camped near an old mine site that had some iron wagons and other equipment left a long time before by whoever had mined there. One afternoon as I nosed around, looking for pretty rocks, old tools, or whatever else might be there, I saw some yellow metal that caught my eye. It sure looked like gold. I was sure it was gold. I picked up several small pieces and ran to my Dad.

"Poppa, look! I found the gold," I exclaimed in my high-pitched voice.

My Dad inspected the largest piece, then bit it, and asked me where I had found it. I took him to the spot which was just beneath the back end of an iron-wheeled wagon. Just above my spot of discovery was a metal box with a corner that had been sealed with the brazing rod.

So I found some yellow metal, but it was not gold. I have used my own homemade yellow metal nuggets to have fun with other people until this day, over seventy years later.

Teresa and my daughters, Kate and Bess with some "yellow metal" they panned from a nearby creek.

On that same trip I found the skull of a large Desert Ram. I persuaded Dad and his friends to let me take it back with us.

A couple of weeks later, a man from the school of mines offered me five dollars for the head, so I sold it.

I found this similar head in Arizona in 1968.

## DONE WITH SECOND GRADE, 1950

One of the highlights for me that summer was getting to drive a small Ford-Ferguson tractor on one of the rice farms, as Grandpa did business with the owner. I just drove it back and forth on a dirt road, but it was my first time to be in control of a vehicle, and a real thrill.

When I awoke each morning, I looked forward to fishing trips to Tres Palacious, Galveston, the Pavillion, the Chicken Pen (pronounced Chinkapen by locals), or other places. We usually caught enough fish to be satisfied and among saltwater fish, I had come to prize "Specs" (Speckled Trout or Spotted Weakfish), Reds (Channel Bass), and large

Croakers most of all. But whatever the fish, I was happy to be trying to catch them. I had my casting technique down pretty well. Then Grandpa bought a couple of Zebco closed-face spinning reels for $9.98 each, and the casting became much easier and with fewer backlashes, but the monofilament line was not as strong as the braided line we used with the older casting reels.

Grandpa's first television set.

Grandpa had the first television set that I ever saw. It was a wooden console model with a small screen of about six or eight inches in diagonal. It was a wondrous marvel to me and almost everyone else that saw it. Grandpa was politically very conservative and any time President Harry Truman came on, Grandpa would get up and turn off the set, as he would not allow that socialistic president to come into his house, even on the television or radio. Grandpa did not swear but his terms for bad people, especially politicians made his feelings clear.

In mid-August, my grandparents took me to California to visit some distant relatives. When we came to the state line between Arizona and California we had some peaches and other fruit with us which the California officials would not allow us to take into their state. We noticed a lot of fruit sitting in paper bags and baskets near the gate and the people

The little Ford Ferguson

working there were munching on the fresh fruit. Grandpa got pretty disgusted with the thought of that guy confiscating our stuff, only to eat it himself, and told the agent that he would not get our fruit as we were going to sit right there and eat it all. And we did. I liked Grandpa's attitude and action, but I didn't have the urge to eat another peach or apricot for a long time.

Grandpa thought we should see Death Valley, so we drove a few hours extra to get there. I decided that place was well named. When I expressed my dislike for the horrible place, Grandpa laughed and told me that he agreed. We just drove through the southern part and we were all glad to get out of the hellish surroundings. That was one place that was even worse than the greasewood country around Socorro, New Mexico, in my view.

We spent some days with relatives in Los Angeles who were raising Chinchillas. I got to hold some of the beautiful little rodents that all seemed tame and friendly. I didn't like the idea that they would eventually be killed so some lady could have a fancy fur coat.

I also was intimidated and revolted by the heavy traffic and people congestion. It was way too big a place for me. I doubted that I would ever be able to catch a fish or hunt any game there. I wanted to be as far away from there as possible, and as soon as possible. I didn't care if there were lots more movie theaters and drug stores in that area.

In San Diego, we visited the zoo. I was interested in all the animals and enjoyed the one whole day we spent there, but I thought those wild creatures must be bored to death to be kept in cages and small pens.

It seemed to me that they were in a prison. It was worse than school, even. I never again had much desire to go to zoos after that experience.

On that long trip, at first, we ate in restaurants and drive-ins most of the time. I sure missed home-cooked meals and told Grandma. Soon after that Grandpa bought a small charcoal cooker, a pot, a skillet, and paper plates. When on the road, he would often look for a pleasant place, and then pull over so Grandma could make us dinner. That was another way of "doing for ourselves" that I liked. Home-made hotdogs and hamburgers tasted way better than the store-bought stuff and it cost a lot less, too. The weather was seldom a problem for our outdoor cooking, except for blowing dust.

From San Diego, we traveled East across a more desolate desert country that I did not care for. We passed through Yuma, Arizona, and saw the old Territorial Prison. I thought that was an appropriate location for a prison and was relieved that we were only passing through.

As we motored East through Arizona, conditions improved somewhat, but none of this area ever approached the verdant beauty of Southeast Texas.

## Back to Work (School) Fall, 1950

Not long after I began third grade, I heard Mom and Dad talking one evening. Dad had received a letter from the army about the possibility of him being called up to go to Korea. Dad was going to the New Mexico School of Mines on the G.I. Bill, he had two children, and he had served three years in World War II, so he was not high on the list for recall. I remember telling him and Mom that I would pray every night that he did not have to go to war again. I worried about losing my Dad for quite a long time, and I Thanked God, every night that he was not called up.

The school gave me back my old crossing guard job and occasionally I could get a little work cleaning up at the feed store nearby. The old cowboy who ran the place liked me and told me plenty of stories of unfenced range ranching and fighting Indians and cattle rustlers, which he called "Ladrones" (which means thieves in Spanish) as I swept the floors. I thought he had enjoyed a wonderful life in the old days of New Mexico and other places he had worked as a cowboy. The old fellow had never raised a family, but he seemed to enjoy being around kids. Mom invited him to our house for dinner several times, where he regaled us all with his stories of times past.

In the warehouse, any spilled grain was carefully placed in a large can which I got to scatter around behind the building for the birds. I was paid fifteen cents an hour and thought it wonderful that in just two hours I could earn enough to see a Saturday matinee ... and have two Big Hunk candy bars (one of which always went to my sister) with a nickel and three pennies left over.- which went into the old sock that served as my bank.

Our "new" used Studebaker.

During the Christmas vacation, we four drove down to a site in Mexico to check out a mine that had offered Dad a job when he graduated. It was the El Potosi mine in the state of Chihuahua. Dad had just traded off the old Ford sedan and bought a used 1949 two-door Studebaker Champion that had a speedometer that measured kilometers instead of miles. It was a much nicer car than we had ever had before and it ran well for the entire trip.

It seemed like we drove for a long time to reach the mine site. I liked the mountainous country, which had snow on the ground when we arrived, but the mine area was not appealing, with lots of old tailings waste that reeked of raw chemicals. Lots of broken-down equipment was lying around. Dad said that the mine produced lead, gold, iron, and manganese, and the area was rich in silver.

The mining company treated us very well, fed us nice meals, and provided a fine apartment for our two nights with them, but Dad thought it did not have great potential and the possibilities of problems with the Mexican government taking it over were real, so he decided he would not take that job.

While still at Potosi', my sister and I both began to break out in pustules. Lucky for us, most of the pustules were on our back, chest, and hairline, so they weren't obvious. I enjoyed popping the little blisters, but Mom told me not to do that, as they might spread or get infected. Mom was pretty sure it was chicken pox but was alarmed at the possibility of the U.S. Border people thinking we had smallpox and maybe refusing us re-entry to the United States. Being stuck in Juarez or any place in Mexico did not appeal to Mom. So we headed north. We arrived at the border town of Ciudad Juarez after dark and we kids were told to act like we were sleeping. We passed right on through, to everyone's great relief. Once back in Socorro, our affliction did prove to be the more benign Chicken pox.

Grandma Nason, my Mom's Mom, had moved down from Iowa where she had been teaching school without a college degree. She divorced Grandpa Nason, who had become an abusive drunk. Gram enrolled in Highlands University in Las Vegas, New Mexico, which was up north quite a ways from Socorro, and in a lot prettier country, to my way of thinking. She wanted to have a college degree so she could teach school in more places. We all went up that spring for her graduation. I wished that Dad could have gone to college there, instead of Socorro.

Gram smoked an occasional cigarette. So, I spent a nickel on a little tin of cigarette loads. They looked like small pieces of a square toothpick. It was easy to stick one in the end of a cigarette and push it up way, so it did not pop as soon as the cancer stick was lit. I really rattled Gram a time or two with those little explosives, but she took it well.

## 1951 Dad graduates and we move back to Iowa

Dad talked a lot about where we might go when he graduated. Newfoundland was a possibility that I hoped he would select, as was Whitehorse in the Yukon Territory. I always favored northern climes. But eventually, he took a job that required him to work in Chicago. My dreams of the wild north country faded. My ears were tuned to hear the call of the wild, not the whispered enemic beckoning of the mild, as would be found in a city. At nine years of age, I had no interest in any large city, or town living in general. So after his graduation as a Mining Engineer, in the spring of 1951, we loaded up the little 1949 Studebaker Champion and drove back to Iowa. I got farmed out, literally, for the summer with an army buddy of Dad's named Roger Morrison who had a small farm near Fairfield, Iowa - not far from Lockridge and New Sweden, where our roots were.

Roger's little farm was a great place. Roger had a son, Dean, that was my age and the farm had a bunch of milk cows, pigs, and chickens. It was my ideal kind of place. Roger had Dean and me milking cows along with him early in the morning and late in the afternoon. He had a separator into which he would pour the buckets of raw milk. Cream came out of one spigot and milk from another. The cream went into a metal can and the milk into a larger one. We would lug the cans into the spring house to keep cool until the local dairyman came by to pick up the milk before noon.

A milk separator machine.

A milk or cream separator is a device that removes cream from whole milk. As a result, the whole milk is divided into cream and skim milk after separation. Cream and skim milk have different densities and therefore they tend to get separated under the impact of gravity.

Milking cows was always enjoyable for me. Their flanks were pleasantly warm but sometimes needed to be toweled off to remove the poop that got on them from their tails swatting flies. I'd stick my head right in the flank and just squeeze away. Dean and I were a lot slower than Roger, but we performed our best, and I noticed how our forearms were getting bigger and stronger. I could see muscle definition developing and I liked that.

There were some small ponds nearby where Dean and I could catch fish,- mostly small catfish that we called mud cats. One afternoon Dean and I found a thick, nasty-looking snake at the edge of the pond. We killed it with rocks and sticks. Then we saw what large fangs it had. We took it home, very carefully with a sharp stick stuck through its large head. Roger said it was a Copperhead and we should never pick up any snake. He threw it in the hog pen and the pigs ate it.

Dean and I had a game we developed that involved throwing corn cobs at chickens. We were playing German soldiers pretending to be throwing potato masher grenades at the enemy. We learned that if we hurled the cobs just right, to make them rotate horizontally, we could knock an "enemy" chicken down, sometimes with a broken neck. We got two hens that way one afternoon, but Dean was worried about what his Dad would say, so he took the dead chickens and put them in the muddy entrance to the barn, to make it look like the cows had trampled them. But, Roger didn't buy that and we wound up plucking the dead chickens and were told in stern terms to quit throwing corn cobs, grenades, or anything else at them. So ended that interesting war game for us, but, fried, the chicken still tasted great.

When the sows were ready to give birth, we would drive those big hogs into their individual pigsties. I was spooked by the huge animals, some of which acted aggressively. Dean told me of local kids that were bitten by hogs and one had even been eaten by pigs, he said. " I ain't had so much fun since the hogs ate my sister," was a common saying in those parts. Roger handed each of us a hardwood barrel stave and told us to smack the hog hard on the end of the snout if one came at us while being driven. We did that and the hogs behaved, but our fear kept us from ever getting into a sty with any of those big sows, however attractive and cuddly as the newborn piglets were. Some of the adult hogs could be ridden, like a horse, so we mounted up and jousted, using broken shovel handles as lances and garbage can lids as shields. We often found ourselves unhorsed (or unboared) and lying in the mud and pig poop, but it was a favorite game of ours.

A young knight without armor aboard his worthy steed.

Roger needed to take his family on a trip, so I got to spend time with some cousins in Lockridge, Iowa. One of my great-grandmas, Grandma Hollander, lived there, too. She always seemed tired and she was a bit cranky. Her house always smelled like old home-canned fruit, but she made wonderful cookies, puddings, and pies.

My cousins, Danny and Wendell had caught a red fox kit and kept it at their house. Those boys set some mouse traps near the fox, which got its paws snapped in the trap and after that, it was not so friendly with any of us. I felt bad for the little fox.

Lockridge had a small drug store with a soda fountain. We loved to go down for an ice cream soda or malted milkshake and would take extra soda straws to later light up behind the barn and pretend we were smoking. Corn silage was easily accessible and we learned that sucking on a fermented corn stalk would make us high. It didn't taste very good, but we thought we were being "big" by doing that.

## Our return to the Great SouthWest - Fall, 1951

That summer passed like a flash and soon Dad, Mom, and my sister, Pat, came to pick me up and they had good news. We were moving to Arizona! Dad got offered a job by the American Smelting and Refining Company (ASARCO, or AS&R) to be the chief engineer of a small, remote mine that produced lead, zinc, and silver.

This time the trip west was easier than in 1947. The car was newer and the tires were too. We pulled a small, two-wheeled trailer with our stuff in it and I don't recall breakdowns on that long trip.

I had been dreading living at a mine in the desert, but this one called the Trench Mine, was back in the mountains of southern Arizona at about five thousand feet elevation and about twenty miles by dirt road from the quiet little town of Patagonia. (I've never learned how it came to be named "Patagonia.") The mine produced primarily lead, zinc and silver, but it yielded a little copper and some gold, too. The mine had been discovered about 1850 when Arizona was still a Territory and worked until the 1940s. A nearby ore body, the Flux Mine was developed and its ore was taken to the mill used by the Trench Mine. The mining company owned eight small houses at the mine site which were rented to higher-placed mine employees who wanted to live there. The houses and mill site were only about six miles across the mountains from the border with Mexico. Those six miles were an all-wild, rocky, ruggged, roadless country. That appealed to me.

Local miners told tales of Apache Indian raids on the mine and nearby small villages, and how Jesuit priests had played a role in the early development.

Trench Mine mill and headquarters. The Trench Mine mill sat downhill from the little house we rented.

Mom and Dad were interested in history and dug up a lot of information about the old Trench mine. This was a "hard rock" mine, meaning that the veins of ore were mined from underground shafts, taken to the surface to crush, mill, and concentrate before being hauled by ore truck to the railroad at Patagonia. Initially, adobe furnaces were used to smelt the silver from the argentiferous (silver-bearing) galena mother rock. The lead was used primarily for bullets. The ore averaged forty percent lead and sixty ounces of silver per ton. By the 1950s concentrates were shipped by rail to the Asarco El Paso smelter.

There were lots of Mexican live oak trees, cottonwood, sycamore, juniper, walnut, and pinon pine trees, manzanita thickets, some Ponderosa pine trees, good grass, and most amazing to me, peaches, apricots, and wild grapes in the area. It was part of the Coronado National Forest. I liked it there, but the mine site houses were all occupied, so at first, we had to rent a house in Nogales, Arizona - right on the border to Sonora, Mexico. Nogales, which is Spanish for walnut, was another town way too big for my liking.

So it was that I entered third grade in Nogales. It was the largest class of which I had ever been a member. And these big town kids were rougher and far more rude than the small town and farm youths to which I was accustomed. There were even some Mexican gangs in this school. From day one until we moved, I frequently got into fist fights.

I had always sort of wished that I didn't have red hair, but I never let it bother me. I felt sorry for those red-headed kids who also were cursed with a face full of freckles. But in Nogales, some of the bully boys liked to call me "pecker head" and say "I'd rather be dead than have red on my head." A couple of times I launched into a bout of fisticuffs over that, thinking I would make them think they were going to get dead, or wish they were if they teased me too much. The teasing seemed to drop off after that. Also, I realized that being called names was not worth much concern.

The old single shot .22 was a breach loader.

Our rental house was on the eastern edge of Nogales where there were lots of huge rocks. Some hills were littered with giant rocks as big as any buildings that I had ever seen. Kids in the neighborhood loved to play in the rocky areas which offered lots of hiding places for ambushes of our opponents in the army or cowboy and Indian games. One afternoon while playing an "army" game, I found a sort of shallow cave formed by a stack of big rocks. We were told to stay out of caves of any kind due to the danger of snakes and spiders, but I eased in, slowly. I couldn't resist exploring that dark recess. Back a short distance inside the little cavern I saw a small, single-shot .22 rifle. The stock was badly broken and the rifle looked very old, but was nearly rust-free. It was a breach-loading firearm. I could hardly believe my eyes! I was glad that I was alone, as anyone with me would claim at least partial ownership of the great discovery. This find was mine, and mine alone

At last, I now had a real rifle, in addition to my Daisy BB gun. When I showed my Dad, he looked it over carefully and told me that we would need to make a new stock, when he got time, then maybe, we would try to shoot it. I could hardly wait.

Within a couple of months or so a house at the Trench Mine site became available and we moved up into those beautifully wooded mountains. The little house was an old frame structure with corrugated metal roofing with the same material on the outside walls. It sat on a hill overlooking the mill, an old tailings dump, and other mine buildings. Off a few miles to the east, the lovely, grassy San Rafael Valley could be seen most days. The little house had three bedrooms and I got the smallest one on the east side of the building. I loved living here. It was my favorite home site of my young years.

Dad and Mom at our company house at Trench Mine

Our furniture was simple, mostly homemade from local materials. Shelving consisted of wooden Hercules Powder boxes built with precise tongue-in-groove corners, instead of nails on the sides. The boxes were stacked and secured by strips of screen molding or whatever wood was at hand to hold the boxes together to make shelves or cupboards. I was amazed that such nice boxes were thrown away by the mining company. Most people saved them for reuse, as we did. Dad made a couch out of lumber and Mom sewed together some cushions made of packing material and covered them with flour sacks. It was inexpensive, comfortable furniture and served us well.

No one threw anything away in those days. Who knew when a can, jar, old inner tube, or anything broken might be just the thing we would need? I still save most good containers.

Grocery sacks were all made of heavy paper and were saved for wrapping items to be mailed. Birthday and Christmas gifts were often wrapped in paper grocery sacks. Nowadays I use them for mailing books or other printed material.

Cardboard (sometimes referred to as paperboard back then) boxes, if in good condition, were saved for future use.

Flour and feed sacks were often made of printed cotton cloth and were used for shirts, dresses, and pants for my sister, Pat. Mom used the sacks for upholstering furniture, and other useful things.

Aluminum foil was called "tinfoil" and was straightened out flat and reused as many times as it would serve.

Mom used an empty Royal Crown Soda bottle as a rolling pin to prepare her pie crusts. She kept another RC bottle with holes in the cap for sprinkling her ironing - it allowed a sort of home-done steam ironing.

Our combustible garbage was burned in an old barrel just outside in the yard.

Jars with screw-on lids were put to many uses. Bottles and cans were just dumped over the hill on the lower side of the yard. I recall how disgusting rancid old catsup bottles smelled.

Dad loved music and often played his clarinet or saxophone during the evenings. I member him playing "In The Mood" often. We had no radio at first, but after some months at Trench Camp, Dad bought a console AM/FM set that gave us all a lot of pleasure and news information. After supper in the wintertime, we would sit by and listen. Not so long after that, he purchased a record player with a "cobra" stylus. This player would bring music out of the common .78 size, the little .45s, and the largest .33 vinyl disks. We had to be very careful to not scratch the record with the needle. Dad especially liked Les Paul and Mary Ford instrumentals and had several records of their tunes.

We were proud of our radio/record player.

Dad and Mom, out of necessity, had been frugal their entire lives but had some debts to pay off after Dad graduated from college. I remember when they told Pat and me that they were out of debt, and again when they had saved a whole thousand dollars in the bank. That was remarkable as I didn't know how much money Dad made in those days, but in late 1955 I remember his saying that his salary was about one thousand dollars a month, which was a significant increase over the previous years. For each of those memorable events, on our next trip to Nogales to buy groceries we did the usual things, bought groceries on both sides of the border, got haircuts and dinner in Mexico, then went back across to Arizona to see a movie. Our activities were about the same as every other time, but the feeling was special, especially due to those landmark financial events.

There were several large tailings deposits near our rented house, some of which were damp and constituted a threat, similar to that of quicksand, so we were sternly warned to stay off of the tailings, no matter what. We generally did avoid them, however, the infrequently badly thrown basketball or softball was carefully retrieved without incident - and without mention to our parents.

So still early in my third-grade year, I was enrolled at the Patagonia grade school. The school bus stopped at the base of a hill about a mile from our house. We walked from home down the hill past the mine's "core house" where the drilling cores were stored, past the "cantina" where the miners stopped by after work for a snort before going home to Harshaw or Patagonia. I never heard of any kid being bothered by anyone from the cantina. In fact, when we did see someone there, the men were always courteous and often gave us a snack of potato chips or peanuts along with their friendly greetings. We walked over a small ridge and down a larger hill to the dirt road which was the main thoroughfare to Harshaw and on to Patagonia.

The bus ride took about thirty minutes and most days the trip was a lot of fun. We had to be careful about where we sat, as the bus driver had chickens that often roosted in the bus at night and pooped on the seats. Kids that boarded late on the bus run had to use a piece of paper or their bare hands to clean off the seat, to avoid getting chicken poop all over their pants or dress. Few people worried much about dirty hands, viruses, diseases, etc. in those days.

As we got aboard the bus a sign stated **COURTESY IS CONTAGIOUS** and most of the kids took that to heart.

Just across the main road from the bus stop and up another short canyon was the old Hardshell Mine, which had flooded and then was used as a freshwater source for the mill and the houses at Trench.

So, if we didn't have other interesting things to do, we could go along the normally deserted roads to visit other old mine sites. I needed a bicycle, as we sold my first one when we left New Mexico. To maximize my coverage of this new country by using the roads, I needed a set of wheels.

In the meantime, the one other kid living in the area and I walked, which led us to lots of other interesting discoveries. His name was Glen. He lived in a mining company house close to ours and was a few years older than me.

There were old mine exploration shafts and diggings all over the place. Wooden head frames denoted a vertical shaft beneath, and we were warned to stay away from them. More than fifty mines had at one time or another been active in the area and countless test holes and pits had been dug and left open. Silver had been the main draw to the area, so of course, we were bent on discovering some silver, or maybe even some gold. We never did find any, but we kept looking.

We, kids, were told to never go into any mine shaft, but of course, the mysterious, unspoken invitation of such places overrode parental advice. We left none of the horizontal shafts we discovered unexplored but we avoided the deep vertical holes. When we stood near the edge of the pit beneath a head frame - also a forbidden activity - a rock dropped over the edge sometimes took a long time to hit the bottom. That was spooky.

Our usual loot was old shovels, worn picks and other worn-out mining paraphernalia, along with skinned knees, torn pants, and bruises. But we healed fast.

## Gyp Joins Our Family

Some time that first winter of 1951-1952, a scruffy little dog turned up in our yard late one afternoon. He was long-haired and his coat was dirty, matted, and ratty-looking. And he was poor - skinny that is. He had pretty facial markings and a long tail. We saw him standing by the back gate and Mom went out with me to see about him.

Rabies was endemic in the region and we had been warned about that dreaded disease being carried by foxes, bats, skunks, and loose dogs, so Mom was on alert for signs of craziness or aggression in the little pooch. When we approached him, he wagged his tail and seemed to smile. There was no sign of foam around his mouth. My heart was completely taken by the little guy .. and Mom's was, too.

When we opened the gate, he came right in and rubbed his dirty coat against Mom's leg. She bent down and petted him and he followed us to the back door. Mom gave him a dish of milk which he lapped up voraciously. Then he wolfed down some table scraps, including even some vegetables. He looked like he hadn't had anything to eat for a long time.

Mom told Pat and me that the dog would need to have a bath, so we got the wash tub filled with warm water and together with my little sister Pat helping, we cleaned him up and brushed his coat. A lot of his matted hair was so gnarled Mom had to trim it away with scissors. The little guy did not resist any of the attention we showered on him. He was calm and seemed to know we were friends.

The dog was fully grown, so when Dad saw him he said we would have to write up and post some notices at the cantina, in Harshaw and Patagonia, in case anyone had lost this good-natured little hound.

That same night I began praying that no one would claim him.

We never heard from anyone, so he became our dog. He had been a gypsy for a spell it seemed, so we named him Gyp.

Gyp fit right in and took to all of us from the first day we met. He slept in my room, often in bed with me. He was housebroken and never, as I recall, pooped inside. One of the ranchers had some rabies vaccine, so we took Gyp for his shot, more to assure Mom than because we thought he needed the shot.

Neighbor kids, Glen and Jerry with their dog, Pat, Me, and Gyp on our porch.

In what seemed like no time, Gyp would bark at wild animals near the yard and sometimes at people. He had a home now and he defended it and us, his family.

And I had a constant companion on my jaunts. Mom liked that a lot.

As we normally were away from home for several hours on our trips to Nogales, we left Gyp in the house alone. When we returned late one night, several months after adopting Gyp, we opened the door to see that he had torn our couch apart. The stuffing was everywhere and the feed sack covers were in shreds. Mom just sat down on one of the kitchen chairs and held her head. Gyp came up to her wagging his tail.

I was scared that this would mean we could not keep the little dog, but Mom patted his head and said that she thought he didn't want us to leave him. Maybe he had been left before he found us. From then on we should take him to Nogales when we go shopping.

We gathered up the stuffing and cleaned up the mess as Mom said she would recover the cushions and have everything back, better than new. It was a big job.

I was relieved and hugged Gyp tight to my chest for a long time before I went to sleep that night.

A year or so later we left Gyp at home and when we came back, we found the couch destroyed again. Mom, God Bless her and her loving patience, said it was our fault and she would re-do the couch again. After that, Gyp was included in all the family trips and he never again did any damage to anything in the house or car. Gyp was our dog and we were his people until he died in 1964 while I was attending Dental School in Portland, Oregon. I miss him still.

## More on Trench camp

Snakes were not numerous in the Patagonia mountains, but skunks were common. We encountered polecats, most often the striped variety, but on occasion, a spotted skunk would be found out in the open or in an old mine tunnel or one of the many abandoned culverts that we crawled through. We generally avoided the nasty-smelling little carnivores, until I started trapping. I set most of my meager supply of traps close to home and checked them every day. Of course, then I had to deal with the skunks that found my leg hold traps and it was never a pleasant chore. Skunks are usually pretty fierce and did not submit to being killed without a fight. The beautiful black and white striped skins were not to be wasted, but no matter how we tried, skunk skinning always resulted in badly tainted hands and clothes. My Mom soon discovered that home-canned tomatoes worked best at removing the smell from me, my clothes, and our dog.

The trench mine ran out of profitable ore in the 1940s, but a nearby ore body called the Flux mine, was found. When the Trench Mine proper ceased operation, the burros that had been used to bring the heavily laden metal ore carts out of the mine were released. The burros survived and thrived on their own. They could best be caught by holding a can full of oats and shaking it for them to hear. We tried using pebbles, but the burros were wise to that - apparently, their oversized ears served them well enough to distinguish the tinkle of stones from that of oats - so we would scrape up oats from around the loading dock of the Patagonia feed store during our lunch hour and take it home in our lunch boxes for capturing feral burros. None of the burros were ornery. Some of those donkeys proved to be willing, cooperative steeds and we put them to good use. A cowboy named Ben, who worked at the mine to supplement his cash flow, showed us how to make rope halters for the donkeys which provided us a means of controlling them when we rode. Soon we found some old horse bits in an abandoned building and then had much better control of our steeds. To keep them close by, sometimes we tethered them on a long line to a stake on a grassy hillside next to the house.

An old lawn mower is a sufficient anchor for a skunk.

We were used to seeing Coyotes on the drive to Nogales, but only on rare occasions did we see or hear one at Trench. When one Coyote yaps, it sounds like a whole pack of them. I still don't understand how one critter manages to sound like so many.

## END OF THE FIRST SCHOOL YEAR IN ARIZONA, 1952

I loved living at Trench Camp. The first full summer we had a nice garden, my sister Pat planted cantaloupes and watermelons, and a few actually grew big enough to eat. We had potatoes, lettuce, cucumbers, tomatoes, green beans, peas, squash, and cauliflower, among other vegetables. Some peach and apricot trees were already there and bearing fruit. Dad and the neighbor man, Sixtus Carlton, did some grafting to make Peach-cots. We had plenty of good water which was piped in from the Hardshell mine, which years before had been forced to close primarily due to underground flooding.

Peaches had been introduced by the Franciscan or Jesuit priests that accompanied Spanish explorers and conquistadores. Harshaw had originally been called Durazno, which means Peach in Spanish. So peaches had been growing wild in the Patagonia Mountains since sometime around 1740 - for more than two hundred years!

The garden attracted birds, of course, and also an animal that I had never seen or heard of before. They looked similar to a raccoon, but locals called them "Chulas", which means cute in Spanish. Some people referred to the little critters as monkeys. I learned that the proper name for them is Coatimundi (*Nasua nasua*). These interesting omnivores traveled in troops and sporadically raided our garden, usually at night. They weren't hard to drive off and I always was glad to see them, despite their depredations which were kept to a minimum due to the noisy ruckus put up by our dog, Gyp. I was told that apparently, the chulas emitted an odor easily detected by dogs, but I never noticed any unusual scents.

The fruit trees attracted Grey Foxes, too, which would climb up into the lower branches of the trees to eat a peach. I'd only seen Red Foxes prior to living at Trench and I was surprised that any fox would climb a tree.

Veterans Market in Nogales, Arizona

We would go to Nogales to shop for groceries and such stuff about every two or three weeks, usually on Saturday. On these trips, we would buy most of our stuff at the Veterans Market, where, as their sign proclaimed, "prices were less and quality was best". Classic comic books cost fifteen cents while Donald Duck and other comics were a dime - Pat and I usually got to pick one or two comic books, each. I was reading all the classic tales and becoming pretty well-versed in good stories. In fact, my familiarity with classic literature which I gained from Classic comic books carried me through college. I could read a Classic comic like the Odyssey or the Iliad in a short time and understand the essence - the moral and message of the story - as well as enjoy the pictures. When I looked at the thick books, most with few pictures, it seemed obvious to me that the best way to enjoy the great classics was by reading the comic book. I read every classic comic book I could get my hands on and, over the years, I read most of them several times.

After the Veterans' Market shopping the family would go across the line to Nogales, Sonora, to purchase some things like sugar, and flour and sometimes some exotic canned items, like abalone. While there Dad and I would get a haircut - I enjoyed the hot lather shave on the back of my neck. We'd have a nice, but inexpensive dinner at a Mexican cafe, see a movie in Nogales, Arizona - I remember one about Captain Horatio Hornblower, with Gregory Peck, then we'd drive home, well after dark.

Often my sister, Gyp and I were sleeping long before we left the pavement at Patagonia and started up the washboard dirt road for Trench. I recall several times waking up in the dark as Dad parked the car at the edge of a dry wash or arroyo that, due to heavy rains was running bank to bank with water and debris. Those "gully washer" flash floods usually took place in August. Sometimes we had to wait for several hours for the water level to drop enough for the car to get safely across the flooding creek and go home.

## Winning the pony

A drive-in movie theater was built in Nogales in the summer of 1952 and the owner held a promotional raffle for a pony with full tack (saddle and bridle) as the grand prize. As I recall, several local stores gave customers tickets for the pony, based on one's purchases. The Veterans' Market was one of the participating stores. From day one, I just knew that pony would be ours! We carefully collected and recorded the numbers of all the tickets we accumulated. Our list was lengthened by donations of tickets from friends of our parents who had no kids.

Time passed slowly as we waited for the drawing. When the big night came, we were all sitting in the '49 Studebaker at the drive-in. I told everyone that I just knew that we would win. Dad said that I should not tempt fate, as we had never won anything in a raffle. Mom cautioned me to not count my chickens before they hatched. But I told them that I absolutely knew we would be the lucky recipients of that pony.

Mom had a list of numbers, Dad had a list, and I held a list. Pat was as keyed up as I, but at age five, did not have a list to scrutinize. When the winning number was announced over the loudspeaker, Mom shrieked that we had it! Dad asked if she was certain. Mom carefully looked again and said YES, we have it! It was the summer of 1952 and I believe that was the most exciting event of my life, up to that point.

We, all four of us, walked (Pat and I were leaping, skipping, and dancing, no doubt) up to the projection building and Mom presented the ticket. The announcer said the ticket was good and announced our names and where we lived.

The Shetland pony was a beautiful black and white pinto gelding and he had a nice, new saddle on his back. It was Saturday night and Dad told the announcer that we could return the next day to claim the pony. The announcer said that would be fine.

We stayed for the movie, but I don't recall what it was. I spent time with the pony and my dreams. And I thanked God for this almost unbelievable gift.

Some kids came up to pet the pony and I could see how disappointed they were and I felt sorry that they didn't get one, too. One boy was just plain angry that he had not won. It seemed to me there was no use talking with him, as nothing I could say would seem right. I also thought a lot about jealousy and decided that the best way was to be happy for others in their good luck and to enjoy my own as it came.

The emotions of the evening had us all completely worn out. When we got home, Dad carried both Pat and me from the car to the house. I woke up when Mom called for breakfast the next morning, but I didn't remember anything from the time we left the drive-in theater until the next morning.

That next morning, Dad, Ben - the cowboy friend from the mine, and I went to the local rancher's headquarters down the road in Harshaw where Dad had arranged to borrow a small horse trailer. The rancher, Norman Hale, was all grins and shook our hand and congratulated us on winning the pony. He also offered to help in any way he could with our new pet.

It was only about eight miles from Harshaw to Patagonia and eighteen miles from Patagonia to Nogales, but that seemed like a long distance to me, especially that morning. Dad bought us hamburgers when we got to Nogales and we arrived at the drive-in to collect the pony shortly after noon. The little cayuse didn't like the look of the trailer and tried to kick Ben. The experienced cowboy was all business and tolerated no nonsense with horses. He forcefully jerked the little pony around and got him loaded. Ben also told us that Shetlands were notoriously ornery and after seeing him kick, we should always be alert for such a dangerous situation. A kick in the head could seriously debilitate or kill a boy or even a man. He told us to always gently talk to the pony, especially when approaching from the rear to avoid surprising it and get up as close as possible, stroking the critter's rump. Close in, a kick would not be nearly so forceful as it would be if we were two or three feet away. He also offered to come over to help if the pony proved to be too "salty" (meaning feisty).

I realized that Ben didn't much care for Shetland ponies.

But I couldn't wait to get in the saddle and at the base of the big hill going up to Trench Camp we unloaded Blazer, as we decided to call him, put the saddle on, and rode him home. Going up the hill he was fine, but when I came to a short downhill grade, Blazer tried to buck me off. The saddle came up in the back and I had to grab hold of the pony's mane to hang on. Ben saw what happened and told us that in addition to the cinch, we needed to put on a billet strap at the back part of the saddle to keep it from coming up like that. He also said the pony was way too fat and we needed to see that his weight was reduced. Cutting his grain to a bare minimum and using him as much as possible would probably do the trick. I figured using the pony a lot would be the most enjoyable chore I ever had to do.

Initially, we kept the pony in the fenced yard. Dad helped me saddle and ride him around every day within the confines of the yard. The pony seemed docile enough, under those controlled circumstances.

A few days later, Ben came by the house after work with a billet strap and put in on the saddle with rivets and leather strapping. Mom invited him for supper and sent a whole pie home with him.

I thought I needed a set of saddle bags, so Mom set about sewing a pair together from heavy canvas. I realized that I could stuff a lot more things into the canvas bags than I could jam into stiff leather ones, so I reckoned that was the way to go.

Pat and me with Blazer.

So, next, we needed a corral and a barn for Blazer. An old tailings pond just below our house had a weathered wooden trestle at the far end. Dad asked permission to dismantle the trestle to get the wood for a barn and the mine superintendent gave his okay.

The old wood was blackened, cracked, dried out, and splintery from standing decades in the hot sun and August rains. Dad and I soon learned just how splintery it was. Mom spent a lot of evening time digging splinters out of our hands with one of her sewing needles. We worked the late afternoons and evenings until dark getting the trestle apart, pounding nails out of the boards, then straightening the nails for use on the barn. Nobody threw nails away if they were usable. We were carrying a load of boards up to our house one afternoon when a neighbor came by with a pick-up truck and helped us haul most of the rest of the wood to our yard.

Dad bought new cross-cut and rip saws in Nogales on our next trip for groceries. He only owned hand tools in those days.

Building the barn and corral was one of those projects that seemed to take "half of forever" to me, but I suppose only about two or three weeks passed before Dad had the little barn done and the corral ready for use. He got it done by working evenings and weekends - and this was before plywood was in common use. We had never even seen a sheet of plywood in those days. Dad had only the splintery, dried-out, wooden planks and scaffolding boards from the old tailings trestle. But he took his time and built that barn tight and, sheathed in scrap corrugated metal, the roof shed water.

He built it about thirty yards down the hill on the south side of the house and it was really a nice addition to our hilltop home. I wish I had a picture of that barn. It had a small shed roof over the side closest to the house, so the pony could stand outside and remain out of the sun and rain. A metal can was fixed to the wall for water. A wide entry Dutch door that was normally left with the top half pinned open led inside to a roomy area large enough for two or three horses. A back slatted wall separated the animals' area from the hay and grain which was stored on the far side. A small feeding bin was just beside the feed storage area. I was so proud of the barn and my Dad, and I thanked God often every day.

Once the barn and corral were completed I had more time to ride that pony. And ride him I did! I made trips to the Hardshell Mine only three miles or so from home and on to Harshaw often. I had to be careful, as the pony would still try to buck me off going down a steep hill ... and he succeeded more than once, but nothing more than my pride was injured. I kept those incidents of me being unseated quiet from my parents. I didn't want Mom to worry.

After a few trips on the road, I grew tired of the same sights, so I began to ride off into the wilder country beyond the roads.

The ground is covered by long grass and loose rocks throughout the area. Blazer did not seem to like the off-road trips and had to be kicked hard in the flanks to leave the roadway, but I wanted to check out each canyon and hill. The pony always seemed relieved to return to a road or trail of any type. He perked up when we were back on the road and headed for the barn. His behavior improved the more I used him.

Riding or walking early in the morning or late in the afternoon I saw more wild game than at other times of the day.

Not long before school started in the fall of 1952 I was out with Blazer looking over some country just south of the main road and up a ways from the bus stop toward the old Lowry mine. I'd heard from people living at Trench that in the old days Mowry produced lots of silver and suffered some bad Apache attacks on the miners and I thought maybe I could find some silver, arrowheads, or something else really neat - maybe even another old gun. That Saturday I left the house right after breakfast and Mom had cautioned me to be careful, especially with the pony, and not go too far. Gyp trotted along behind. Blazer never tried to kick Gyp. It seemed they were tight friends. Well, it was a nice day, I had a sandwich and a bottle of water in one of my saddle bags and a small pick hammer in the other, but I did go much farther than Mom would have been comfortable with. After all, I was past ten years old and thought I knew the country pretty well.

Coes Whitetail deer were common in the area. We saw deer often from the house and when driving on the road. I had been picking up every antler and skull that I saw and longed for the day when I could shoot a deer. That morning, about an hour's slow ride off the road, I saw some patches of deer hair on an open grassy slope surrounded by brush, so I rode up as close as I could get before getting off the pony. The hill was steep, so I dismounted on the uphill side - a much easier offloading for me, but I always got on and off on the pony's left side. I tied the halter rope to a stout manzanita branch and began looking around in the long grass. After a short search, I saw sun-bleached white bones, then I spotted the skull of the Coes deer buck laying near the base of a large oak tree at the edge of the open grassy area.

It was the head of a dandy Coes deer buck.

The antlers were larger than any I had seen before. Hide and hair remained from below the eyes to the top of the skull, but had been torn off around the nose. The ends of the nose bones were chewed off, too. I could detect a little smell, but it wasn't too bad. I was determined to take it home. When I approached Blazer with the head in my hand, he snorted, wheeled, and lunged away, loosening the halter rope. As he tore off down the hill littered with loose rocks I was worried that he would fall and hurt himself. The bridal reins were trailing along from his bit to the ground and I feared he would step on one and fall down head first. I was feeling really worried as I tried to catch up to the panic-stricken pony, but I held onto that dandy deer head.

The next hour and a half, I spent trying to catch my pony, but every time I would come close, he would snort and lunge away. Finally, his route intersected the dirt road where he turned left and headed for the hills of home. Gyp stayed right with me.

I was wishing I could get hold of Blazer at least long enough to get my sandwich and water bottle out of the saddle bags, but that was not to be. My belly was cramping with hunger pangs and my mouth was dry as dirt. I bent over and scooped up a handful of water from a small stream by the road, but it had a chemical smell to it, so I did not put it in my mouth. There was a lot of mine pollution in the area and most of the creeks were bad.

I told myself that I would just have to ignore the discomfort and not think about how hungry and thirsty I was. That really helped and I often did similar in future times of pain or discomfort.

It went on this way until we were back up the hill and on the road near the cantina. Luckily Blazer knew the way home and the security of his barn. He had become experienced at not stepping on his trailing bridle reins.

As the pony came trotting toward the little saloon, three miners stepped out and managed to get hold of first one rein, then the other, and held him for me. He kicked a time or two at the strange men, as he was apt to do to anyone. As I neared, Blazer snorted again and reared up. One of the men told me that the deer head must be scaring the pony and I should put it down. Reluctantly I put the deer's head on the ground and got hold of the reins. One of the men said it was a really big Coes buck and, from the look of it, had been killed and eaten by a mountain lion. I told them that I wanted to keep that head. After some discussion, the men told me that the bartender said he would hold onto the head for me and I could come to pick it up after I got the pony back home and in the corral. So, with the men restraining the pony, I got aboard and rode as fast as I could go back home. Blazer was more than willing to gallop that afternoon and he didn't try to pitch me off when we came to the downhill swale. I got the saddle off, placed it over a rail, watered the pony, and ran back to the cantina to retrieve my deer head. As I knew kids weren't allowed in bars, I hollered from the door and the bartender chuckled a little as he brought me the head. He and another guy drinking from beer bottles said it was from a really big deer. As I headed home elated at my luck of finding the deer head, I felt really tired, so I just walked slowly.

One of the finest homes I visited in Harshaw sits deserted sixty years later. (It was the James Finley House, which was buillt around 1877 as a residence for the superintendent of the Hermosa mine.) I snapped this photo in 2014, long after the house had been abandoned.

Knowing I'd gone further than I was supposed to, I told my parents of the events of the day. Mom said she was disappointed that I had gone so far and that such a trip was always a risk. What if I had been hurt and the pony came home alone? Where would they begin to search for me? What if the lion had attacked me? There were other "what ifs" as well. In the end, I agreed to write down where I planned to go on a little chalkboard that Mom kept in the kitchen - it was a flight plan, of sorts.

When Dad saw the deer head and heard my story he told me that we had better plan to go deer hunting when the season opened. That made all the frustrations of the day well worthwhile to me.

After I was in bed, I remembered my sandwich was still in the saddle bag, so I snuck out to the barn and got it. Soggy and mashed or not, I could always eat it tomorrow. It looked like a big ball of fish bait but tasted just fine.

That was not the first nor the last time I had to walk home, following my spooky, unruly pony.

Often I rode the pony down to Harshaw, where most of the residents were Mexicans, many of whom worked at Trench Mine. Often I was offered treats such as tamales, empanadas, sopapillas, and tacos. I developed a preference for that food, as long as it wasn't too spicy and hot. I still crave Mexican food and eat it often.

The older Mexican men told me stories about how bad the Apaches were, coming through that country on raiding parties, often killing people and sometimes kidnapping women and children. I suppose their stories were based on facts, as some of the men looked old enough to have been around during the times of Indian raids. I kept an eye out for any Apaches that might still be hiding in the hills, but I never saw any, but as recently as 1930 Apaches had raided Harshaw and nearby mnes.

There were plenty of Mountain Lions in those hills and lions fed primarily on the deer. We occasionally found Cougar tracks but never saw a lion around Trench Mine.

A Jaguar was killed northeast of Patagonia in the Santa Rita Mountains that spring and that got everybody's attention. Mom said it would be awful if I got eaten by a lion or a jaguar. Yeah, I thought so, too, but I had no intention of discontinuing my exploration of the wild country. We heard reports of black bears but never found a sign of any in the 1950s.

Javalina, or Collared Peccary, were native to the area. Those little omnivores had a horrible reputation for ferocity, but always ran away when I tried to approach them. The largest boar might tip the scales at fifty pounds. The three Kolbe brothers at the Rail X Ranch captured two javelina piglets one summer and the little hogs became pretty sociable with humans. On hot days they would come up to us, stick their noses under our pant legs, lift the pant up, and lick the sweat from our legs. Walter Kolbe, Senior had us picking and pitching rocks out of his fields often, so we came in pretty sweaty and the pigs loved that. I was never scared of Javalinas.

## Fourth Grade, 1952

With Trench located only six miles from the border with Mexico, we sometimes saw people coming through the country with small packs on their backs. Locals called them "wetbacks", probably because Mexicans that entered the country illegally around the Rio Grande River sometimes had to swim to get across. Sightings were common enough that nobody got too upset about it, but people did report things being missing. One of our neighbors said their chicken house had been raided and several good hens were gone. We figured wetbacks had done it, but no one was ever caught.

After one of our shopping resupply trips to Nogales we came home just before dark to find some unfamiliar Mexican-looking people - I guess we were profiling - but such natural practices were considered to be common sense in those days - the strange Mexicans were tearing apart the front porch of our house! Dad drove right up to the gate, bailed out of the car, followed by Mom, and ran through the gate at the thieves. I got out of the backseat as quickly as I could and joined the chase with Gyp yapping along. The gang of thieves looked like a family with a man, a woman, and four kids my age and older. They scattered like a flock of quail. The man ran out of the yard and was side-hilling through the oak trees toward the barn. I was in the yard above him and threw a large rock at him. The rock was bigger than a grapefruit and I had to use both hands to throw it from over my head. The rock struck the running man in the small of his back, knocking him down, but he yelled, got up, and kept going.

Dad saw what happened, ran over, and grabbed me. He said if I had hit the man in the head, I might have killed him. I nodded my head, and enthusiastically said "Yeah, Dad". Then Dad picked me up, took me to the barn, bent me over the rail, and gave me a paddling so furious that I couldn't breathe for a while. I thought that I might suffocate. It was the most serious spanking that I ever got. Dad said that no matter what was happening, no one should ever lose their senses and overreact. If I had killed or seriously injured that man, I would be in far more serious trouble than the thief. I didn't think any thief deserved one bit of consideration, but I never forgot that whipping - or Dad's message.

School started in September and I enjoyed it more than ever. Teachers, kids, and everyone seemed friendly and fun to be around. The bus ride to town was always a lot of fun. Most of the kids were older than me but treated me nicely. One girl who was in high school boarded the bus before it got to our stop. She was several years older than me, and very pretty and pleasant, always. I thought she liked me. I tried to sit next to her whenever I could. She smelled good. She teased me some, in a nice way, so to even things up, one day I asked her if she would marry me. I was only teasing, but she recoiled, and then laughed.

"Well, yes, I might, if you grow up and turn out to have promise", she said - or some such thing. But she didn't tease me as much after that - and I missed her attention. I wished I hadn't asked her the question.

The school was an older building that had been well-built and maintained. In fact, I visited the site in 2013. It was still in use and still in top shape. It sits atop a large hill on the northeast corner of town. There was a large swing set in front of the school. It had chains that suspended the seats from the top rail. We boys had a bail-out competition which involved getting the swing going as high as possible, then bailing out. Whoever could make their heel marks the furthest won the match. My heels would get so sore I had to walk on my toes, but I liked the game. Of course, we boys thought of ourselves as practicing up to be paratroopers.

30 Patagonia Grade School looks the same - 65 years later

We played softball in the area behind the school. One recess period as I slid into the third base I felt a sharp poke on my hand and found half of a beautifully made arrowhead, with serrated edges. The teacher let me keep the arrowhead and told the class that an Indian village had once been there. After that, we all kept our eyes peeled for arrowheads and several more were found, along with bits of broken clay pottery.

That fall Dad began to plan our deer hunt. I asked about the stock for the rifle I had found in Nogales. He fashioned a piece of hardwood so that it fit me just perfectly. The next afternoon he put a .22 short in the breach, secured the rifle to an oak tree in the yard, and pulled the trigger with a string. It fired! He said I could carry it when we went hunting, but that it was too small a bullet for a deer. The barrel was only sixteen inches long, so its range and accuracy were not the best, either. But it was my first "real" rifle.

I found the arrowheads one at a time.

Soon after moving to Trench, I noticed that neighbor Glen had a Daisy pump BB gun which seemed more accurate and better than my old lever action, so I soon made a swap with a kid in Patagonia and upgraded to the pump model. It proved to be a much better bird and lizard-getter. I think I had to give the kid a whole dollar and my BB gun for the swap.

The pump was much better than the lever action BB gun.

Mom and Dad's rules were that I had to properly use whatever I killed, as the killing was only to be done for a purpose, and never just for fun. Most of the birds of whatever species I shot, from robins to sparrows, got cooked and eaten - and they all tasted great - and about the same, but Mom did not like the notion of having a lizard (some of which were not at all pretty) in her pans, so I would buy a quart of rubbing alcohol, place my lizards in a clear glass jar and cover them with alcohol. I was preserving my specimens for future scientific study, of course. When my collection grew too large for the little porch, I had to move the jars out to the barn.

When deer season finally opened, we would get up before daylight, have a quick breakfast, and head out. On school days we just walked from the house and came back in time for me to catch the bus and for Dad to walk down the hill to work. On weekends Dad would drive the little two-door Studebaker to more distant places. We began each day as the sun came up, sitting in a place from which Dad could use his "field glasses" (binoculars) to survey a good amount of country. He sat patiently glassing, while I shivered in the cool of the morning. I never could figure out why it got coldest just before sunrise, but I sure noticed it.

Several times Dad located and pointed out a legal buck deer to me, which was always exciting, but he did not get a shot at one while I was with him. One afternoon while I was still at school, Dad and another miner saw some deer as they drove back from the Flux mine. He had his German 8mm Mauser with him in the company truck and, after a short walk from the road, he got a three-point buck, which was hanging from a limb near the back door of our house when I got home.

When I saw the deer my whoop was surely loud enough to be heard 'round the world. I ran my hands over the sleek grey carcass, and marveled at the long tail, so white on the underside. Dad came out the door, and asked if I would like to help him skin the deer. Of course, I was more than ready to do that. It didn't take long for us to remove the skin, which I wanted to preserve - forever. We rubbed some table salt on the skin and hung it over a pole in the far corner of the yard. When I went to check it the next morning it was gone. Most likely a fox had pulled it loose and drug it off. Of course, I allowed that maybe a mountain lion or even a jaguar had done it, which was much more exciting than a mere fox.

Some snow patches remained in places and the temperature was plenty cool, so Dad decided to hang the carcass for a couple of days to "age" the meat by hanging it inside the screened porch.

He used his cross-cut wood saw to remove the antlers and skull plate from the head. The antlers were tacked over the door of our house. Mom took the tongue and made it into a soup, along with flour dumplings. I even liked the deer liver fried up with onions. Normally I did not care for liver.

That most beautiful of all deer was the subject of discussion on the bus ride to school the next day.

For Christmas that year I got a new K-bar sheath knife and Dad gave me his own single-shot .22 with a long barrel. I was ten years old and gearing up for the next deer season.

---

We had a phone at the house at Trench camp. Of course, it was a party line and we had our own unique ring code of long and short bursts from the bell. None of us used the phone very much, but often when we picked up the earpiece we could hear others on the line. That was a signal to hang up and try again later.

## The Rail X Ranch

In third grade, I made friends with Jim Kolbe. His family owned the Rail X Ranch which was located north of Patagonia, towards Sonoita. I was often invited to the ranch for weekends. We got along very well. Jim who was three months younger than me had a brother, John, who was about a year older, and another brother, Wally, who was four years older. His sister, Beth, was two years younger, as I recall. From the beginning, Beth didn't like me at all.

By fourth grade, on weekends at the ranch, we usually had some work to do, often it was picking rocks up from the fields prior to spring planting. Usually, John would drive an old dump truck from the headquarters site down the road and into whichever open field was to be picked that day, and then he'd get out and help Jim and me toss rocks into the back. Occasionally John would let Jim or me drive the big truck for a little while if it was in a field and not apt to hit anything. I enjoyed that work, sweaty and dusty as it was. It was a bit less interesting than gathering chicken eggs, cleaning the chicken and cattle pens, and feeding the cattle and horses, but still, it all was enjoyable to me. Walter Kolbe Senior would give me a dollar or two sometimes, as well, but that didn't matter as much to me as just being on the ranch. Wally was usually off doing other chores appropriate to a young man of his age and experience. He got the chore of repairing flat tires in the tractor that had a flat due to running over shed deer horns.

The ranch was a working cattle ranch and had a Dude Ranch (Kolbes referred to it as a Guest Ranch) component, as well. A really fancy house was up on a hill overlooking the working ranch headquarters and was called Casa Rosada. It had a swimming pool and when no guests were lodged there, and the work was caught up sufficiently, sometimes we kids all got to use the pool, as a special reward. Usually, Mrs. Kolbe, Helen, would accompany us to ensure safety and keep the horseplay to a tolerable and safe level.

Once as we walked down the little creek from Casa Rosada to the headquarters someone saw a small snake. All the kids were spooked, but I decided to catch it. When I got hold of its tail, it whipped around and bit me on the left forearm. I got bit three times before I had it under control, but the bites were not serious and I had conquered my fear of snakes - right there, in front of everyone. None of the other kids wanted to hold or have anything to do with that little serpent, so I just released it back into the grass. I suppose it was some variety of garter snakes. My snake bites showed small tooth marks, only one of which bled a drop or two. My arm healed up fast, and with no complications. We all decided it was best to not mention my action with the snake to any adults.

Wally, being older, was a hero to all of us. He played football on the six-man Patagonia High School team and was admirable in every way. He had his own room and often would invite us younger boys to listen to his records. I remember one of the favorites - "Istanbul was

Constantinople, now it's Istanbul, not Constantinople, so if you've a date in Constantinople, she'll be waiting in Istanbul." John and Jim shared a room and when I overnighted with them, the three of us stayed up until late telling stories and playing games in their room. If I stayed over until Monday morning, I caught the bus with the boys along the paved road that ran close to the ranch. I so wished my family had a ranch like that one. Any ranch would do. This bus had a different batch of girls, some of whom I thought were cute.

Supper time was always an opportunity - more like an obligation at the Kolbe table - for political discussion. Kolbe's were conservative Republicans, as were my family members and the discussions and debates at mealtime were enlightening and often quite noisy.

Mr. Kolbe, Walter, Sr., began referring to me as "Jake" to avoid confusion with his son Jim. Many of my relatives had acquired the name and I liked it. That name stuck with me.

None of the Kolbes had any interest in hunting. In fact, I recall them cussing deer when a shed antler would puncture a tire, necessitating a patch. It was especially upsetting to Wally when it was a large tractor tire that needed to be removed and a patch placed on the damaged tube. That sort of chore was usually done by Wally working alone.

There were always a lot of house cats around the ranch headquarters, which seemed to fend for themselves. Mrs. Kolbe and Beth would put out scraps from the dinner table and pour some milk into a pan for them, but most were too wild to come near people. When the cats began to bother the chickens, Mr. Kolbe told us that we needed to weed most of them out. Wally, John, and I got to use a pump .22 repeater rifle to shoot cats, but only if we were careful to not hit any livestock, vehicles, or buildings. We did shoot a good number of barn cats and did not damage anything else.

We, kids, were expected to act responsibly, and we did.

We spent several days shoveling and spreading some sort of salt mixture around the bottom of some artificial depressions that had been dozed up to hold water. After the ponds were full and proved they could retain water, Mr. Kolbe arranged to have some Blue Gill sunfish and Large Mouth Bass put in the ponds and I was allowed to come to fish. Wally loaned me a lure called a River Runt which he guaranteed would catch bass .... and it did. That fishing was a real draw for me and Wally, but it seemed no one else was much interested in it. Sometimes my Dad would drive me down from the mine just to fish. I thought the fish all tasted good, mostly because I had caught them.

The main house and most of the rest at Rail X had very thick walls made of adobe and covered with some kind of plaster inside and out. The old cowboys told us that all the older houses had been built in the 1870s and had such double thick adobe walls because that would stop bullets during Indian raids. They told us that renegade Apaches passed through that area frequently and were not averse to killing white people, along with their favorite victims - Mexicans - as they went about their primary goal of stealing horses and cattle. I never missed an opportunity to listen to those old cowboy and Indian stories and wished I had been there at the time. If I had been around back then, I was sure I would have been a rancher, rather than a miner. And I liked the idea of hunting down bad Indians. What an adventure that would have been!

To my mind, a farm life would be really good, but a ranching life would be ideal.

In 1954 Twentieth Century Fox shot a movie called "Broken Lance" in the area and leased Casa Rosada for parts of the filming. I got invited to go to the ranch for a day of filming and was kissed on the cheek by the lead actress, Jean Peters. I didn't wash the lipstick off, ever. In fact, I went over the marks with Mom's lipstick to preserve them for as long as possible. I got to shake hands with grumpy Spencer Tracy, amiable Richard Widmark, kindly Robert Wagner, Hugh O'Brian, and Earl Holliman. But Jean Peters was the one person that impressed me the most. Some years later I read that she had married the millionaire Howard Hughes and quit making movies.

I remember riding to church with the Kolbes in their big touring car that had an extra set of seats that folded up for use in the middle of the interior. The news that day, as we were going to church was that the French Foreign Legion had fallen at Dien Bien Phu. It was in May of 1954. All of us boys talked about joining the French Foreign Legion to fight the evil communists.

## In Patagonia, Fall 1954

Probably due to his family's dinner discussions, Jim Kolbe was keenly interested in politics. There had been widespread jubilation in November of 1952 when General Eisenhower was elected president and most people were full of patriotism and love of the country. At school, we pledged allegiance to the flag every day and sang songs of all the different armed services - off we went into the wild blue yonder, and struck out from the halls of Montezuma. We also sang "Dixie", "When Johnny Comes Marching Home Again", and the Battle Hymn of the Republic. We were all proud to be Americans, and we realized how blessed we were. I believed then and do now, that a strong sense of patriotism and nationalism are necessary and healthy for all Americans - probably for people in other countries, too. It's healthy to be proud of your country.

The first week of fifth grade our homeroom teacher told us we should elect a President and other officers of the class. Jim Kolbe told me that he wanted to be President of the class and, eventually, President of the United States. I told him that I would vote for him, but I was more interested in going hunting or playing marbles, in fact, doing almost anything other than being a political figure, was my dream for the future. When Jim wanted me to be his Vice-President, I agreed but took no interest in school politics, which for me, simply translated to more indoor meetings with lots of people, which dealt with issues in which I had little interest. Most of the "problems" were in the minds of the people right there, not most of the folks in the area. In long meetings, I could feel my butt going flat and numb. I wanted to be outdoors and not in a crowd, or in a meeting. Grandpa Jacobson used to say of political controversies, they were - "jest like bugs a-fightin." I agreed with that.

So that was my friend Jim Kolbe's first successful election. He went on to serve for years both in the House and the Senate of the Arizona State Legislature, then several terms in the U.S. House of Representatives.

## CAPTURING AND RELEASING THE SKUNK 1953

My friend, Glen, who lived next door at Trench Mine was already in High School, but since I was the only other gringo kid living in the vicinity, he sometimes took me along to share in his adventures. One Saturday a high school classmate of Glen's named Max came to spend the day. Max was driving his Dad's old pickup truck. We immediately realized the truck would make a long-range exploratory trip a tempting possibility. None of us could resist the temptation of that or almost any other expressly forbidden pursuit.

But Max had not been to Trench Camp before and he was interested in all the old mining stuff nearby. Glenn and I had located and crawled through most of the wooden culverts associated with the old mill just below the houses. Most of the culverts were of short length - maybe one hundred yards or less. We'd found one, which was a bit larger in size that permitted a fully erect hands and knees crawl down the middle. It would be easier than a belly-sliding transit, which was necessary for many of the culvert explorations. This tunnel had some cables and wires on the floor and tacked along the side walls. Glen and I had only partially spelunked this big, long culvert. We had turned back due to the dank darkness that lay beyond the first turn. Max wanted to be one of the first to make the trip. He mentioned Sir Edmund Hillary climbing Mt. Everest, Richard Burton and the discovery of the source of the Nile. He mentioned Lewis and Clark on their great voyage of discovery, and other great deeds. (In those days public schools taught history.) The thought of emulating the great explorers spurred us on. It occurred to me that I'd never heard of any great explorers who crawled through man-made culverts to their destination. Ours might be the first crawl of discovery, I reckoned.

We would need flashlights for this one. After some desperate searching at Glen's and then at our house, we scraped up four "D" cell flashlights and set off for the big tunnel.

Max, who was the oldest and most eager for fame, took the lead. Of course, I brought up the rear. I was reminded of the first joke I ever heard, way back in first grade involving three moles going down a mole hole.

Papa, Mama, and Baby Mole. Papa Mole said "I smell honey". Mama Mole said I smell honey, too." Baby Mole said, "Ugh, I smell mole asses." But I was determined to hang in there. Max and Glen didn't smell that bad to me - yet.

We pulled our pants up as high as possible, tightened our belts, and began our somewhat less-than-grand exploration. For some reason, we whispered, rather than spoke in our normal voices. Subliminally, I guess, we kept our voices low because we knew that we shouldn't be engaged in that unnecessary, dangerous, and clearly forbidden activity.

In places where the weight of the ground on top of the culvert had resulted in a leaky and sagged depression, the floor was muddy, but we wormed our way around the fall-ins and water puddles and crawled on. There was a musty stink throughout. After the first curve, we could see no light at the end of the tunnel in front or behind us. Then I was glad to be the last in line. We began to encounter piles of rocks where the roof and fallen in, but we intrepid stalwarts crawled over the debris which was encumbered with wires, cables, and occasionally nails. We inched our way on, into the unknown. We began to wonder how far the tunnel would take us and to what end. Might we wind up in Mexico? The border was less than six miles from the mill. I began to feel uncomfortable, but I had faith in the leadership of Max and Glen, after all, they were high schoolers, and I could always squirm around and go back out the same way I had come - as long as my flashlight lasted. We had not encountered any snakes or large spiders, which was a relief to me.

The air began to smell even worse - a musty, chemical stench, it was - but we hunched along. After what seemed like half of forever and another curve, Max said he could see light up ahead.

We crawled on, hoping - even dreaming of finding some sort of Shangri-La with beautiful girls ahead. Normal, adolescent boys are that way, I guess.

By the time I could see the light through the arms, legs, butts, and other human body obstructions in front of me, the air smelled much worse. I knew the essence of skunk!

"Hey, theres a skunk in front of me!", Max announced, this time yelling, not whispering.

Glenn reversed gears, jamming his butt in my face and nearly taking me off my four-point stance. I pushed back with my muddy hands.

Max had already sustained a partial shot of skunk spray and hollered that he needed a stick to prod the striped polecat on toward the light, which was faintly visible in the distance.

I had been noticing loose boards at the top of the culvert and pulled one loose that hung down between Glen's butt and my head. I got the wood loose, but it brought with it a fall of rocks and dirt. Then I got scared that we might be buried forever in that dark shaft. What a miserable sepulcher that would be! When our bodies were recovered - if they were ever found - we would all smell like a skunk! I had a spooky vision of Mom bathing my limp and lifeless body with home-canned tomatoes.

I passed the board up to Glen, but it had rusty nails protruding from both ends and Glen got a deep scratch on his forearm. He hollered some profanities my way as he passed the board up to Max.

The skunk was waddling its way forward, toward the light and freedom, but would occasionally turn, stand defiantly, and then turn again, raise its hind legs, and let loose another blast of repellent juice.

The athletic performance of the little stink beast brought images of high school cheerleaders to my mind. But we in the audience, weren't cheering.

The piece of board was about thirty inches long, not long enough for the job of prodding the skunk, but it was all we had available.

I was sure glad that Max had been so intent on placing his name at the top of the discovery notice. Now he was paying his dues, wearing the awful odor, for sure.

Glenn and I began to cough from the stress, fear, and stink. Our progress seemed slower than molasses, but finally, the skunk was out of the culvert and we three budding adventurers quickly followed.

Ah, the daylight and fresh air, tainted as it was by the malingering essence of skunk, was most welcomed by us all.

The little boar skunk stood on his toes and remained feisty.

During the squirming over the last sixty yards or so, Max had dropped his flashlight, which both Glen and I had failed to notice. No one wanted to go back to look for it.

Once outside we assessed our situation. We were on the edge of an old excavation dump that overlooked a steep canyon. The skunk, which

I saw clearly for the first time, was a Striped Skunk - and a big one, too - was posed at the edge of the precipice. We all smelled like skunk, big time, already, so we had little to lose.

As the skunk was still nearby and should be about squirted out, Max said we should catch it and take it to release in the high school ventilation system. This guy was a thinker!

Max took off his now oily-looking, stinking, Levi jacket and told Glen and me to help surround the critter so he could get in close and throw his jacket over it. That mission was accomplished with relative ease, after only a couple of misses. Once enveloped in the jacket the skunk calmed down. I knew from skinning a few of them and looking at their skulls that skunks were capable of delivering a savage bite, so I did not ask for a turn holding the captured beast.

Oh, how nice it was to be in the fresh air, contaminated as it was with the skunk smell emanating now more from us than from its manufacturer.

We trudged on up the hill, got on a road, and walked to the truck.

Periodically the skunk would thrash its legs and growl, sort of. We surmised that the old Levi jacket would not hold its live contents all the way to Patagonia, so we liberated an empty wooden Hercules powder box from Glen's Dad's tool shed, carefully placed our live prize inside and, over its vocal protests, snapping jaws, and flailing claws, we nailed the lid shut.

We were hungry. Lucky for us, Glen's Mom was visiting over at our house, so we snuck into Glen's kitchen and made up some jam sandwiches to sustain us on the next leg of our project. The sandwiches tasted kind of funny, probably due to the skunk juice on our hands. Glen's Dad, named Sixtus, drank Schlitz Beer, so Glen grabbed one can for the trip. I had sipped beer before and didn't care for the taste, so I filled my water bottle, and without a word to anyone's parents, we struck off for Patagonia in Max's pickup with the powder box containing the skunk in the back. Needless to say, we left the windows wide open and had the side vents open, too, to enable us to endure the pervasive odor. Max and Glen shared the beer and threw the empty can out the window just before we got to town.

Down the road past Harshaw, we stopped at a small ranch and hollered up a kid named, Bucky, to allow him to share in our activity and glory, but when he got a whiff of us, he said he had too many chores to do. He would not even get close, to the pick-up. I had always figured Bucky was a smart kid.

As soon as we reached the blacktop road, just west of town, an old fellow who was a neighbor of Max's waved for us to stop, so we did.

"What have you boys gotten into? Oh, never mind, I can smell it," was the old guy's comment.

Max said we had to go.

"Well, you kids be careful now, ya hear?" the old man advised.

It was mid-afternoon on Saturday, so the high school was deserted. Max backed the pick up close to the door at the back of the building and finagled with the door until it opened. Glen and I carried the powder box behind Max and pried the lid off when we found the big ventilation duct. It was overhead, so we had to thrust the box up to it. Without hesitation, the skunk charged down the new passageway. I can still hear the clicking of its claws as it scampered down the galvanized tin duct, rounded a corner, and was quickly out of sight.

Max said he hoped the skunk would generate a lot more stink juice to thoroughly aerate the building by Monday morning. The pole cat had a day and a half to do that. Max and Glen speculated on how they would be heroes when the whole school got an unexpected vacation, due to the smell. I remembered my tadpoles from back in first grade. In a few short years, I'd progressed to the level of pole cat.

Max figured we had better clean up, so he went to his house and got some homemade white lye soap (my Mom and other women of the day made their own soap out of lard and lye) which was normally just used for washing clothes. Then he drove us to Sonoita Creek south of town. We peeled off our reeking clothes and got into a pool with the caustic bar of soap. We tried to de-stinkify our clothes, then put them on bushes to drip dry. That soap nearly peeled our skin off, but it did not take most of the smell with it - from our clothes and our hides. Of course, Max was the most contaminated of the three of us, but the difference was by then, hardly noticeable.

It was a warm day, but as the afternoon sun got lower on the horizon we got chilly, so we put our still damp, stinky clothes on and Max drove us back to town.

Grandpa and Dad had warned me that handling a fish that I intended to release too much would remove their protective slime and could lead to their sickness or even death. I never liked bathing too much and figured that my natural protective crust was an asset. After this lye soap scrubbing, I knew I was completely devoid of any such protection. Heck, my hands and arms were beet (or beef) red and chaffed to the point of bleeding in some of the overly scoured places. My knees were the worst, probably from crawling that long distance on the rough and splintery culvert boards.

I had some secret thoughts about how maybe hanging out with older boys might not be always the best idea, but despite the smell, it had been a really fun day. And I felt grateful - even honored to have been a part of it all.

Max grabbed a handful of hard candy and some pieces of fried chicken at his house which we snacked on as he drove us back to Trench. We three made plans for more adventures as soon as possible. A thorough exploration of a deep mine shaft seemed like a good future venture. And it seemed we had a winning team, or so Max declared.

He let Glen and me off at the main road bus stop, so as to not alert anyone that we had gone very far in the truck. Glen and I quickly walked the mile uphill to home, giggling and congratulating ourselves on our big caper.

Well, as could be expected, Mom sniffed me and knew right away that I had been fooling with a skunk again. I was just plain worn out, but I knew that I had some explaining to do which could not be postponed.

When Mom got a whiff of me, she told me to go outside to the yard and tell her how I had gotten into skunk trouble this time. Dad came into the kitchen when he heard the discussion.

Knowing that crawling through the old culvert would get me the worst reprimand, I got that over with right away. I left out the part that it was the largest, longest, and darkest of the abandoned culverts in the area.

Dad said he had told me plenty of times to never do such a thing as I could get killed and maybe never be found if the top of the abandoned culvert gave way. He said he was going to discuss this with Glen's Dad, too.

Mom asked why my clothes were wet and mentioned that it looked like I had tried to use white lye soap on them, as spots of the white soap showed on my clothes. I told her that we tried to wash up in the creek, but I didn't say we had gone all the way to Patagonia and Sonoita Creek.

Mom asked what had become of the skunk and I told her that we released it, still alive, but I didn't say where, and my innocent parents neglected to ask. She mentioned that she couldn't understand why three seemingly normal, smart boys would ever want to capture a skunk alive, anyway. I told her that since we were already sprayed, we may as well try to catch it, just like Frank Buck in his "Bring 'Em Back Alive" book.

My Dad tried to not laugh, but I noticed him stifling a snicker.

Thinking that no one would ever connect us with the skunk in the high school ventilation system, I left that part of the story unsaid.

Mom gave me my supper on the front porch steps and right after I ate the hurried meal, she rolled up her sleeves and opened some jars of home-canned tomatoes from our garden. She brought out an old galvanized wash tub and told me to strip off my clothes and stand in the tub while I rubbed the tomatoes all over myself from head to toe. I figured Glen must be going through the same humiliating treatment in his yard.

Poor Gyp. He stayed right with me but did not rub against me. He obviously was repelled by the smell.

My little sister, Pat, just grimaced and went to tend her cantaloupe plants.

Dad walked over to Glen's house to discuss our activities - especially crawling through the culvert, with Glen's Dad, Sixtus.

My fatigue had vanished but soon revisited me as I stood naked and wet in the dark near the back door. Wow, was I ever tired! And I noticed that I had some new holes in my britches and some pretty nasty scratches on my knees. The skin on one's knees is tough - tough as a woodpecker's lips, I imagine - so the splinters didn't penetrate far, and they were not difficult to tease out with a sewing needle.

Dry clothes felt good, but I still had to hand wash those skunky pants, my shirt, and my Levi jacket. I used the tomato pieces and juice in the wash tub, then began scrubbing them with lye soap, using a scrub board and a new tub of water. My hands were red as beets from the caustic soap, but I was confident that some Corn Huskers' Lotion, Bag Balm, and a little time would bring them back to normal.

It was fully dark when I had the clothes ready to hang up on the line. They still carried an unattractive odor.

Our faithful little dog, Gyp, stayed with me, but he hung back somewhat, no doubt due to the odor I still carried.

Mom gave me a glass of milk and some cookies and I went right to bed.

But Mom woke me early the next day, as we were going to church. Following the service, we went straight home and she had a bunch of chores for me to do. It was payback time for my transgressions of the day before, I figured.

It was a good year for acorns and the big oaks in our yard had dropped a lot of the little nuts, along with leaves and other stuff. Most of the acorns had little worm holes in them - what a shame or I would have tried to eat some. I had to rake the yard and haul the junk to our burn pile, but I got to torch the pile and stand by as it burned which made the chore almost worthwhile to me.

Next, I had to scrub the outside of the house, removing cobwebs, dust, and whatever else might blemish the appearance. I spent the entire afternoon doing chores that otherwise might have been left undone. I wondered if my sentence would go on forever - a year, ten years ... maybe I'd get a life sentence.

Monday went much as usual for me at school and I told no one about the skunk escapade. But I was pretty sure that other kids could still smell me. Jim Kolbe told me he knew I must have caught a skunk, but he assumed in a trap, so I did not give him any details.

At lunchtime, we heard that the high school had shut down for the day, but not why it closed. I had a pretty good idea of why.

So, a day and a half was time enough for the skunk to recharge his sprayer and test it in the confines of the air duct system. I wondered if skunks enjoy their own smell.

Before the first kids got to school, the janitor had detected the strong essence of skunk and sounded the alarm. As a lot of the kids lived out of town and were not expected home until late afternoon, the school authorities directed the student body to do things outdoors that sunny day, as they went about investigating the smell and figuring out how to rid the building of the causative agent as well as the irritating odor. Lucky for all, it was a beautiful day and outdoor athletic practice made the time go quickly. It was a bonus event for everyone, except for the two old men of the janitorial and maintenance crew.

Word was, that some savvy person told the maintenance man to use a house fan to blow smoke through the ventilation system to drive the skunk out. It worked and the harried striped mustelid shot out the same entrance by which he had entered, and ran down the hall, squirting as he ran out the door, with claws clicking on the floor and into the wild. I'll bet that skunk had a story to tell!

The smoke added to the noxious odors pervading that institution of higher learning.

But even after hand scrubbing accessible areas and using spray chemicals throughout the ducting, the skunk odor remained noticeable for weeks. Kids and teachers just had to learn to tolerate it. Strangely, I felt secretly proud of that.

That Monday evening Glen was not on the bus to return home, but he often stayed late at school practicing his pole vaulting and other athletic skills, so I didn't think anything was amiss.

Mom told me to clean the barn and corral, so that took up my time until supper.

But at supper time Dad told me that Glen and Max had been given a week's furlough from school - they were suspended for the skunk prank. How the school officials ever found out, none of us boys could figure, but find out, they did.

Dad knew the grade school principal, one Mr. Butler, - well, everyone knew everyone else in small towns back in those days. He called the man on our party line telephone to 'fess up for me and learned that the principal already knew of my participation in the prank and planned to summon me to the office the next morning - right after the Pledge of Allegiance. When Dad hung up the phone I was sent out to pick loose rocks out of the road going up the hill to our house. I made that job last until nearly dark. I decided that my partners in crime must have ratted me out ... but I comforted myself with the thought that they probably didn't mean to implicate me, they were probably caught off guard or something, or so I told myself. Then again, it could have been the old man we talked with on the way into town, or maybe Bucky had mentioned how bad we smelled. Loose lips had sunk our ship, no doubt.

I expected a whupping before bedtime but did not get one.

So Tuesday morning arrived way too soon for my comfort, but just as the principal had told my Dad, I was called to the office, escorted by my homeroom teacher, whom I sensed didn't much like me, anyway. I thought he was coming along just to enjoy my suffering. But, I reminded myself, I was eleven years old and could stand and take as many swats as might come. I was mentally braced, but nevertheless, dreading the punitive backside reward for my grievous behavior.

The principal, Mr. Butler, a rotund man with an undersized shirt that looked ready to pop the buttons off at any moment, and always showed his hairy belly button, had a flare for drama. He glared at me when I entered his small office, then went back to writing on a piece of official-looking paper. I knew he was sweating me, trying to make me squirm. I thought of Yuma Prison. Maybe he was writing up papers to send me to jail. I sure wished I had a chance to talk with Max and Glen to see how dire their comeuppance had been. Briefly, I thought that since I hadn't seen either of them since our skunk enterprise, maybe they both had already been hauled off to prison someplace. Could they do that to kids, I wondered?

After dragging out the suspense, during which I was left standing and due to cramps, had begun to shift from foot to foot, finally, the Principal loudly smacked his pen down on his littered desk, raised his head, and glared at me again. It seemed he was waiting for me to break - maybe whimper or make a sound or say something, but I kept quiet and looked him straight in the eyes.

Straight, unblinking eye contact had always been considered a virtue in my family, so I was well-practiced in that.

Then he broke the unnerving silence.

"Mr. Jacobson, do you have anything to tell me about how a skunk got into the ventilation system at the high school ?" he asked.

I was backed up against the wall, both literally and circumstantially. I just told him the truth and assumed full responsibility. I even pointed out that it had been a Striped Skunk, not a Spotted Skunk, not that it made any real difference, but maybe those adults didn't know much about skunks and this revelation might somehow re-focus their ire, or at least distract them some.

I figured if I tried to blame the older boys, I would never get invited on any more of their adventures, and that - being left out or labeled a squealer - would be a fate worse even than a beating, or prison.

"So, it was your idea, then?" he asked.

Well, to my great surprise, my homeroom teacher interceded on my behalf and made the point that no pair of high school boys would be that strongly influenced by a mere eleven-year-old fifth grader.

"Mr. Jacobson, are you the leader of that gang of miscreants?" the Principal questioned.

"Well, no Sir, I'm not the leader, but those guys let me go along with them and they listen to what I have to say, too, and we usually have fun and don't ever hurt anybody, or vandalize anything" was my reply. I had only been on that one excursion with the older guys, but I hoped for more and this was my opportunity to show that I deserved some respect, even from older guys.

Once again, my homeroom teacher stepped in and told the Principal that I was a good student, had straight A's, and never shirked a job or responsibility that came my way. I did extra work at school and had once even offered to sweep up the room after a messy day. He had seen me stick up for smaller kids when a big local bully was abusing them. And, I was the Vice President of the fifth grade. All of which was true.

As I stood there, the thought of offering to help de-stink the high school had occurred to me, but with the teacher doing such a great job for me, I decided to just hold off on that offer, at least for the time being. The memory of scrubbing my clothes with Mom's lye soap was not a pleasant one and working in the ventilation duct would surely require more such work on my clothes. My hands were still red and sore from the multiple scrubbings two days before, despite repeated and liberal use of Corn Huskers Lotion and Bag Balm.

After some minutes and several contemplative "Ummms," the Principal stood up and told me that he wanted to hear me promise to never put a skunk in any school ventilator or any other part of the school again.

I was dumbstruck. Is that all? Not even a dozen or more swats?

"Now, I want to hear you make the promise," boomed the Principal.

"Mr. Butler, I promise to never put a skunk in any part of the school, ever again," I dutifully responded. I was already thinking of other things like bees, ants, tadpoles, a snake - the possibilities were limitless, but Mr. Butler hadn't thought of them. This was just too easy. Can school teachers be that dumb? Surely more punitive pain must be coming my way.

Then we shook hands to seal the oath and my teacher and I went back to class.

Since I got no paddling at school, I got none at home, either. That was another huge relief for me.

Word of the skunk action and my words with Mr. Butler got around school and the town, nearly as fast as lightening - or maybe the speed of smell would be more appropriate. Other kids seemed to like my handling of the situation. I got nods from some adults, while others just slowly shook their heads when I passed.

Later that week, I was down by the old train station playing marbles at lunchtime with Paul Showalter when Max drove by. He stopped the truck and motioned for me to come over. He said that he was enjoying his week vacation from school and that he and Glen had been chewed out pretty hard for leading me, a youngster, into a life of crime, but my responses during the interrogation conducted by Mr. Butler had eased things for them and he suggested that we get together for some more fun sometimes. I told him I was ready, anytime he wanted to, but I'd had to promise, that no more skunks go to the school, however, that still left plenty of interesting opportunities for us, like snakes, spiders, bats, etc. I favored bats for our next escapade. Max nodded affirmatively and drove on.

## AUTUMN 1953

Before deer season opened, Dad got out the old double-barreled shotgun and we went Dove hunting. Mourning doves were common in the area, with a few of the larger, white-winged doves mixed in. Doves fly fast and are small, so they make challenging targets. Their meat is dark and tasty. I referred them to the Gamble Quail which had dry, white meat, and Quail guts smelled bad. Soon, it became apparent that the most effective way to hunt doves of either species was to conceal ourselves near a water source that the birds were using and wing-shoot them as they came in. As Dad had only the old twelve-gage double gun, which had way too much recoil for me, my job was to watch one way while Dad watched the other. I would tell Dad when I saw birds coming.

Hearing of locals using .22 rifles to pot shoot doves on the ground, Dad, somewhat reluctantly, allowed me to do so, but he said I was to never try to shoot a bird sitting on a high wire, either telephone or electric service. If the bullet severed the wire, fire or worse could result. For sure a .22 bullet hitting a wire would require some expensive repair work and that alone was reason enough to not do it. So I promised to never do it. If any landed close by on the ground or a low branch, I could shoot them with the single shot .22 short, but I should aim for the head, not waste the meat, and I had to be sure there was nothing in line with the shot that could be accidentally hit.

This type of hunting was not as exciting or as tiring as walking for deer or rabbits, but it was interesting, nevertheless, and I liked eating the dark meat of the doves.

We never got a lot of doves around Trench, but we drove a few miles to different places, saw new areas, including the beautiful, grassy San Rafael Valley, and learned the location of a lot of water holes. The depressions dozed or dug out by ranchers to hold water for their stock were called "tanks" and those places were the most productive for us, but concealment was often difficult. The areas near the tanks also were a great source of current information about the big game, too, as the mud held tracks of deer, javelina, or whatever else might have come by for a drink. This sort of information gathering was far more interesting to me than reading a newspaper.

Cottontail rabbits and the larger hares, called Jackrabbits, were scarce around Trench, but we often saw them along the road at lower elevations. A long drive for a dove hunt sometimes provided me with the opportunity to shoot a cottontail or two with my .22 rifle. Everyone in our family liked fried or baked rabbits better than chicken.

So, the dove season served to get us prepared mentally and honed our marksmanship for the upcoming deer season.

When opening day finally arrived, Dad had arranged with the school for me to be absent for hunting. Permission for such absences was taken for granted in the rural communities of Arizona in the 1950s. In addition to the quest for supplemental meat, deer hunting was a cultural tradition that few dared deny and it seemed that most everyone participated in the hunt, even for some of the ranchers who viewed deer as a nuisance critter.

We had been doing some scouting for Coes deer evenings and weekends before the season and Dad had picked two spots within a short drive of the house that seemed most likely to produce a buck for us.

I was keyed up and dreamed of a big buck coming our way.

We got up plenty early, had a big breakfast, put our sandwiches in the lunch boxes, and struck out in the Studebaker. Down the road we drove, then turned right, heading south toward Duquesne. Dad planned the trip so we would be on the East side of the mountains when the sun came up - the side favored by deer in cooler weather. About a mile and a half short of Duquesne, we saw some tents and cars, and lots of noisy people. Several hunters from someplace had set up camp. We had never before seen so many hunters. Dad drove on down past the ghost town of Duquesne, and it was after sunup when he parked the car and we walked up a hill to glass for animals. We saw no deer that morning, but we heard several shots.

For the evening hunt, we went to our other "hot spot" and saw a few deer, but none were carrying antlers.

As we drove home, Dad could see that I was disappointed, so he explained to me that we were hunting on public land and every member of the public had the same right and reason to be there. Without public land, only land owners or people they invited could hunt. Without public land, ordinary people would either have no place to hunt or they would have to pay a bunch of money to go hunting. So, along with the good aspects of being able to use public land, we had to accept the fact that sometimes it would be already occupied or too crowded. That made sense to me, but I still wished those strangers had not come to "our" land.

Territorial instincts are part of me and every other human, I figured. Dad opened a can of smoked oysters as a rare treat for us.

The next morning we set off walking from the house and Dad had a three-point buck on the ground before two hours had passed. He shot it as it stood at the base of some sheer red rock cliffs. The buck was clearly hit, but it charged downhill and disappeared into some thick manzanita brush. When we got to the spot, a lot of blood was on the ground and we found the deer without much trouble only a short distance away. We had to drag the gutted carcass down into a steep-walled canyon. Of course, once at the bottom, we had to drag it up the other side. This was not the most fun part of deer hunting, but I sure would rather be doing it than not having the deer. For most of the trip out with the deer I carried Dad's big rifle as he did the real work. A short piece of rope tied to a stick made the job easier. I learned that you just never know how a day will turn out, but it pays to keep trying.

## Appendectomy 1953

Following the Christmas break, I developed a severe belly ache. At first, Mom thought it might be due to so many cookies and slices of fruit cake, or the gobs of gravy I coated on everything. However my midriff pain persisted for more than one day, so I was taken to the local physician, Dr. Delmar Mock, in Patagonia. He said I had acute appendicitis and should have my appendix removed. He said that he would need to do that in a real hospital, so arrangements were made for my surgery at the Catholic Hospital in Nogales.

Needless to say, I was not too keen on having my belly slit open, even if it was to be sewn up right afterward, but it looked like there was no other way out of this unhappy situation.

We all trusted the kindly Dr. Mock. My folks were calmly supportive of his diagnosis and they assured me that I would be good, or better than new shortly after the operation. Yeah, sure, I figured. Oh well, I could tell the kids at school that I had a serious incident with a guy who used a knife. Let them think of robbers and murderers if their imagination took them there. I would enjoy that.

Most vividly, I remember the early morning cold in the operating room and the ether. It was my second encounter with that awful anesthetic. In my dream, I was trying to holler HELP, but I couldn't get the HE to join up with the LP. That was weird. One of the nuns who worked as a nurse told me that she thought that during surgery, I was trying to cough, or laugh, as I kept saying ... Heh, Heh, Heh.

Well, I sure wasn't laughing, but I didn't admit that to the nun.

I awoke sooner than the doctor expected, in an austere hospital room, shared with two other surgery victims. Both were old men and both spoke very kindly to me. One even offered me a chew off his plug of tobacco which I thought was licorice. When I took a bite, it tasted awful. I nearly threw up, and that hurt a lot. A nurse rushed in and held a pan to my face, but I didn't upchuck, I just hurt. Mom came in about that time and hugged me, which made me feel a whole lot better. The power of a loving hug is amazing! She asked what that awful smell was - the plug tobacco did have a remarkably bad odor. The two old fellows remained silent and I elected to not mention what had caused my nausea. Nope, I was never one to rat on anybody.

For the next ten days, I remained in the hospital. For the first couple of days, I was mostly reading books until I began feeling better and devised new means of entertainment. Someone had loaned me a Classcs Comic book of Herman Melville's Moby Dick. When I read of flensing the whale blubber I became uncomfortable, thinking of the lance that must have been used to flense open my own hide.

On day two, by happy circumstance, Glen, from next door at Trench camp had his appendix removed and was placed in the same room. The two old men had been released. Then I was given the use of a wheelchair which was a lot of fun. As soon as he could move without too much pain, Glen talked the nuns into letting him have a wheelchair too, so we two recovering invalids used our new machines to race around the outdoor patio that connected the patient rooms. Though he was older and stronger, I beat him a time or two, until he caught up with the healing. The second time we were caught racing, we were denied the use of the wheelchairs - forever.

We figured we'd been excommunicated or some such thing.

Those formerly kindly nuns had become semi-hostile to Glen and me. The older "brides of Jesus" were especially down on me and my neighbor friend, casting stern glances our way every time they came close.

When I went home I was supposed to take it easy and not ride the pony or a burro for a month. Dreading the thought of popping my guts out all over the back of my mount, I reluctantly complied for about a week. That time was pretty boring, but I healed up without any complications.

As a side benefit, I was proud to show my new scar to other kids. I told the gullible ones that I got it from a guy with a knife.

Glen, the athlete, was not so compliant with the regime of reduced activity and had some minor complications with his healing, but in the end, he came out fine and went back to his pole vaulting.

## SPRING BATS 1954

Bats were plentiful around Trench. They were seen especially at dusk and dawn in the spring and fall. They were so graceful and beautiful when flying around the yard catching insects, but up close their faces were mean-looking. I think all kids and most adults are scared to death of bats. Bats are also notorious carriers of rabies.

I was told many times to stay away from bats. But, like snakes, they fascinated me.

One evening a bat turned up on our porch step. Gyp, our dog, found it first and began barking. When I went out to see what was causing him to sound off I nearly stepped on the little bat. It was unable to fly, so, without touching it, I used a stick to push it into a small cardboard box. I kept one hand over my face to prevent the mini vampire from flying right up and biting me on the nose, which was a nightmarish image that leaped into my consciousness. When it tried to climb up the sides of the box, it soon fell back. It acted sick, and I felt sorry for it, but I saw no froth around its mouth, so I thought it must not have rabies. It sure had some dangerous-looking, sharp canine teeth and opened its mouth wide to show them off. Its face was as mean and scary as I had ever seen on any animal - or movie. And it never smiled. That was a very effective scare tactic that made my hair feel like it was standing straight up. I thought I should try that - show my teeth - next time I got in a fight, and hope none of my teeth would get knocked out! I laid a board over the top of the box and set it near the door to show my folks when they came home from visiting the neighbors.

By the time Mom and Dad got home, the poor, hideous-looking, little bat was dead - probably from stress. I wanted to check out its teeth, stretch and tack out its wings, and properly investigate it, as I had never before been this close to one. But Mom flatly refused permission for me to do anything but get rid of the infernal little beast, as soon as possible. I could see there was no use arguing with her on the matter.

It was time to burn some garbage, so Dad put the bat box on top of the pile and let me torch it off. My fascination with fire had diminished some, but I still liked to manage the garbage burning.

Not long after that bat incident, as I did my morning walk to the bus stop, I noticed some small bats flying into a hole near the peak of the roof of the old core house that sat down by the cantina. I surmised that they must be roosting inside the old building during the day. That evening, just before dark, I rode Blazer down to the core house and sure enough, several little brown bats came zooming out of the hole near the peak of the roof and were gone in a flash.

Now my curiosity was thoroughly aroused.

Thoughts of those interesting little bug catchers kept re-entering my consciousness. They were mammals, like me, and could actually fly. Grandpa often told me that our family motto was: "If you think you can, or you think you can't, you're probably right."

Maybe I could fashion some sort of wings modeled after theirs and try to fly too, I reasoned. Where Leonardo DiVinci had failed, I might succeed. Being able to fly would be so handy. Just thinking about soaring around looking over the country, hunting for deer and all was intoxicating. But I needed to see how their wings worked. I sure wanted to check one out, but I dreaded the thought of the thing latching onto me with those sharp teeth and, worse yet, giving me a case of rabies. I didn't like the thought of having to go back to the hospital due to bat bites. Even worse yet, I'd heard the rabies shots were all given in the belly and were the most painful of all injections. I couldn't imagine how those old nuns would treat me if I wound up back in their care due to such a foolish transgression. Foolishness is akin to sin, I figured. But I kept thinking about flying.

When we next went to Nogales to buy groceries, I had an inspiration. A new shipment of oranges had come with the fruit in orange mesh bags. They were big, thick-skinned oranges - Navel oranges, I was told. I pestered the folks for some and they bought a large bag.

My sister and I ate an orange on the way home and I debated whether I should take the bag before we had eaten them all. That might reveal my plans. On the one hand, I wanted to make the delicious oranges last for a while, but I needed that mesh bag for my bat capture plans. By mid-afternoon the next day, a Sunday, I emptied the oranges into a wicker basket and snuck the bag off to the barn.

It wasn't hard to fashion a catch net. I cut a piece of an oak branch with a fork in it, threaded the two ends through the top of the orange bag, and secured the ends of the sticks with some baling wire. It made a fine bat-catching net. But with my school and chores schedule, I would have to wait for the next weekend to put my plan into action.

One nice aspect of "the plan" was that I could operate in full daylight, as that was when the bats would be roosting. The core house, or almost any building for that matter, was super spooky after dark.

But how would I get into the core house? I checked it out one afternoon on the way back from school. A large padlock secured the front door, and the creaky old back door was latched from the inside. Breaking into or entering buildings without permission was forbidden - that went without saying - but this building just had old drill cores in it and was seldom visited by anyone - and I wasn't going to steal or damage anything. Nevertheless, it was going to be a scary undertaking, fraught with the real possibility of a serious whupping if I got caught. But considering all, I decided it was worth the risk.

I tested the badly weathered back door and it easily came open about an inch or so. I could see that the inside latch was just a simple cabinet hook. I lifted the latch hook with the blade of my pocket knife. Every normal boy carried a pocket knife in those days. It wasn't difficult. As I eased the door open it scraped the bottom over the old flooring, and I was in!

Once inside, I realized that I would need a flashlight. In the dim light, I could make out the isles of racks with shelves from the dirt floor to the ceiling. The racks were loaded with old drilling cores. It looked like I could climb up those racks as easily as using a ladder. Everything was very dusty. I could see some light near the front of the room at the peak of the roof, but it was too dark to distinguish any bats. This was a really spooky place. I suppressed my thoughts of tarantulas, scorpions, werewolves, or other evils lurking amongst the cores. Most of the cores were 3/4 inch in diameter. Lots of broken ones littered the floor, so I pocketed a few.

When I went out the back door a disturbing thought dawned on me - how was I going to latch the door when I left? I couldn't figure that one out, so I pulled the door closed and left it unlatched. Beginning my career as a burglar was not without its unanticipated problems. I was uncomfortable with the image of myself as a burglar, but then, I wasn't stealing anything, so I decided to go ahead with my project. The lure of scientific investigation trumped my fears of acquiring a criminal reputation.

My plan would require the bat net, something to hold the captured bats, and a flashlight, and I decided to wear gloves - just in case a

**101**

bat tried to bite me or a spider got me on the hand as I climbed up the racks. Anyway, I realized, this was not going to be a job without risks.

Frank Buck must have had plenty of problems catching African wild animals, too, I reminded myself. But old Frank kept at it. So I would too.

Saturday finally rolled around and when I woke up it was raining hard. I decided to wait for better conditions. The next day was dry, and the folks said we were not going to church in Patagonia, so my plan was a "go". Dad was helping a friend with a car problem while Mom and Pat were off baking cookies at a neighbor's house. I was home alone and on my own.

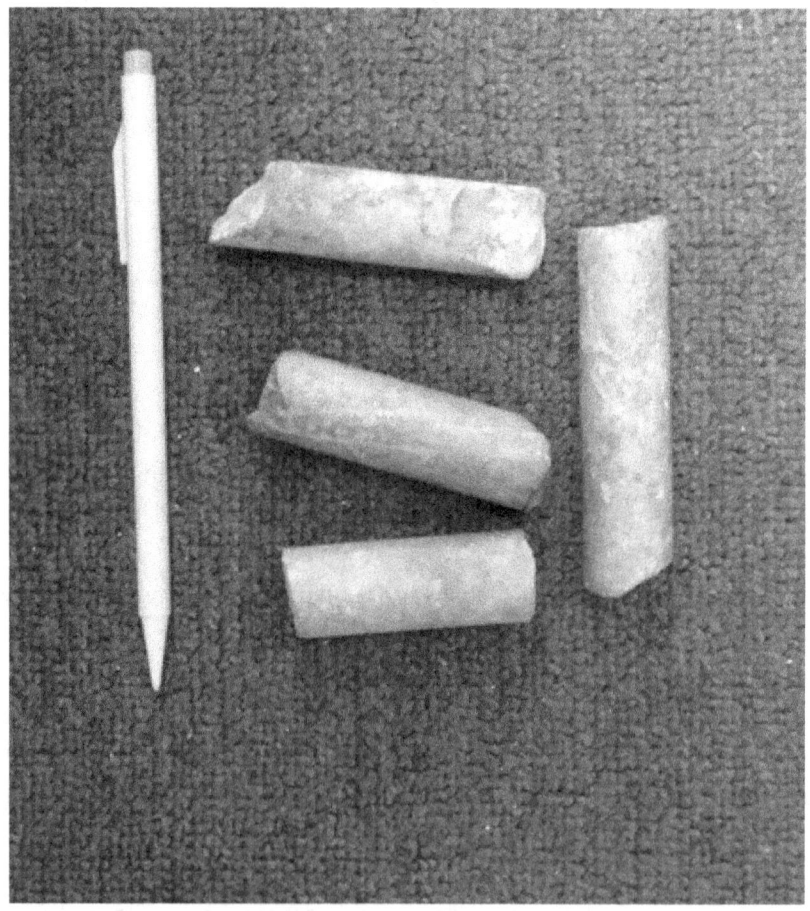

Drilling cores

With the potential of encountering a rabid bat, I left Gyp at home. I knew if a ruckus started, Gyp would be right in it, defending me. The thought of losing that fine little dog to such a horrible disease as rabies was too dreadful to think about - especially if it was my fault that he got bit.

Gathering up my gear I walked down the hill with the net, a flashlight, and a large glass jar with air holes in the lid to hold my captive bat. I wore a pair of Dad's thick leather work gloves.

Despite my reservations about this project, I was determined to try to safely capture a bat without damaging its delicate little body or wings or injuring myself.

When I got inside I flipped on the flashlight and located a bunch of hanging bats right away. There were lots of them - it looked like more than a dozen - and I thought I could hear them squeaking. It was like a little tick, tick, tick sound. It was a bit unnerving, but not so bad as the long crawl through the culvert with Max and Glen had been. It was probably not as scary as the screech of a mountain lion, which I had never heard, anyway.

Before I could even begin to climb, the air was full of flying, ticking, bats. They were headed for the hole at the peak of the roof. Rats, I had forgotten to block their exit! I accidentally dropped the flashlight and gave the net a big scooping swing and felt something hit it. I put the net on the floor and laid a chunk of rock core on the base of the handle. And something was struggling inside that net! As I headed for the exit I stumbled on my flashlight and fell down next to the back door. Getting to my feet in a bit of a panic, halfway expecting a troop of tarantulas or scorpions to attack me, I opened the door wide to let some light in, and seeing no cavalry of nasty arachnids assembled, I went back to the net. Three of the hideous little vampires were tangled in the web and they all seemed angry. With their mouths wide open I could clearly see their sharp white fangs.

Pulling the gloves on as snugly as I could, I gingerly took my prizes outside. When I grasped the first one it immediately bit at my glove, but got its teeth tangled, so, as I held the net down with one foot, I carefully gripped the bat by its back with my other hand and placed it close to the jar. When it disengaged its teeth, I released it into the jar. The next one went about the same. Afraid that they would not have enough room, I held the last bat in my hand and tossed it in the air, letting the third wannabe vampire go airborne.

The little bats were feisty and spooky as could be.

Phew! I was tired already. It must have been the stress.

After getting the door pulled shut I sat down to look at my bats. They had calmed down but were glaring at me. They were breathing rapidly. Fierce little guys, they seemed defiant, rather than afraid. I admired their attitude.

Then I was struck by the memory of the animals I had seen in the San Diego zoo, separated from their natural pursuits and freedoms, they were surely doomed to death by boredom. I could not think of a worse way to go.

After a few minutes of feeling sorry for those little bats and bad about myself, I removed the lid and poured them out onto the ground. One of the bats crawled to the corner of the building and began to climb. I prodded the other to follow along. When they reached the eve of the roof, first one, then the other dropped off and flew away. And I began to feel a lot better. Walking home I wondered if those bats would recognize me if we ever met again.

Bringing 'em back alive, I discovered, had a downside that was not for me. I wished I could share the emotions and events of my semi-successful endeavor with my family, but I decided to keep this episode to myself, and in the future, I would try to be more thoughtful in my choice of projects.

At dusk one evening a week or so later, as I rode Blazer past the core house with Gyp following behind, I saw several bats. Two of the winged hunters swooped close by me making their clicking noises. I figured they must be saying thank you. And that really made me feel good. I knew I had done the right thing by letting them go.

## 1954 Silver Bell

My aunt Hazel, the oldest and sweetest of Dad's sisters had come to visit. She was wonderful to be around, and always happy. She had that special kindness that can best be described as the "Peace that passeth understanding", - kind of like my Dad, Mom, and both my Grandmas showed. Nothing ever seemed to get her down.

Another Mining Engineer, named Bob Kupsch, who worked for American Smelting and Refining Company, (ASARCO) came by for dinner one evening. Even as kids my sister Pat and I could see that something positively clicked with Bob and Aunt Hazel. They both seemed to just glow in each other's presence. There was magic at work. I think this was the first time I recognized love in the eyes of adults, other than my own Mom and Dad.

Dad and Bob were going to take a jeep to explore the area around a property owned by ASARCO north of Tucson for a few days and they asked if I would like to go along. Of course, I wanted to go. The trip would be during the school week, so Dad called Mr. Butler, the grade school principal, and got permission for me to be absent. It was just a formality, but Dad believed in being thoughtful like that. I kind of felt like Mr. Butler deserved the courtesy too, as he had been fair with me on the skunk episode.

The property was located West of Tucson and driving up the sand washes and dirt roads, it seemed like a long way to me. It was hot, dry, and really dusty, and the country was full of creosote and jumping cacti, or cholla. The cactus didn't really jump, but it was so easy to get some stuck on your clothes or skin, the cactus seemed to just jump into place. I'd seen a lot of cacti, but never such seemingly alive, aggressive sticker bristling plants as these. It was as if they just sat motionless until they saw a chance to leap out and stick something - and it was often me.

There were also huge patches of prickly pear cactus in some areas, some of which were chewed up by something. They had a moth-eaten appearance. Wild pigs (Javelina) must have done it, we realized.

As we were driving the jeep up a soft sand wash, we turned a sharp corner and were in the midst of a large herd of Javelina (Collared Peccary). I'd never before seen more than ten or twelve of those little wild pigs in a group, but we counted more than twenty-five in this mob. They were on both sides of the jeep and ran back in forth across the wash. They seemed confused, more than frightened or aggressive. I thought I heard growling when a big one stopped near the jeep. Then they were gone. We had not taken Gyp on this official company business trip and it was just as well that he had missed the meeting with the bunch of wild hogs. Gyp would likely have attacked them and maybe been chewed up himself. Javailna were known to attack dogs, especially when defending their young.

Dad said that they were not actually pigs, but some other type of critter, but with those hog noses, they were pigs to me.

There were old shafts, some rusty iron-wheeled carts, and other signs of abandoned mining efforts, but the country reminded me too much of Socorro, New Mexico, with cholla cactus instead of creosote bushes. I appreciated Trench Camp even more.

Not long after that trip, Bob invited us all to have dinner with him and Aunt Hazel in Nogales. A few months later, Bob became our Uncle Bob when he married Hazel. I was pleased to gain that very nice guy as a member of the family.

In a few short years, Silver Bell mine was developed in the area we had explored and, suddenly, a whole town - with a MacDonalds, a movie theater, and all, grew up out of that desolate desert. After about thirty years or so,(established in 1954 and abandoned in 1984) I heard that the mine was pretty well played out, people left to seek employment elsewhere and many of the houses were loaded up on trailers and hauled off to other towns. Glen, who was working as a firefighter in Tucson bought a couple of houses and put them together to make a really nice place for his family.

Back in those days, when there was no longer any work, people left and a new ghost town was born. No governmentt counseling agency set up shop to help people deal with their grief. No government agency swooped in to support the out-of-work residents, as is common in the United States now.

It seemed to me that the mining business was prone to boom and bust cycles often resulting in ghost towns, whereas farming and ranching were more stable. That was another reason I did not intend to become a miner.

## FALL 1954, 6TH GRADE

This was to be my last year at the old school on the hill. Kids from seventh through twelfth grade attended across town at the Patagonia Union High School. That sounded exciting to me. And the skunk smell had pretty much worn off.

About a month into the new school year, Dad told us that he had bought the Texaco Service Station in Patagonia. His job at the mine allowed him enough time evenings and weekends to run the small station and he had enough experience in keeping automobiles running to do most any repair jobs that came his way. Grandpa Jacobson had done a similar thing back in rural Iowa, along with tending his farm.

The idea of us owning a business was neither here nor there to me, but I soon learned that Dad had located a small rental house close to the station so we would have to be moving to Patagonia. Living in any town was not good news as far as I was concerned. Mom thought the bus ride was a bit long for Pat, at her young and tender age of six years, so moving had Mom's full support.

At the dinner table at Trench Mine, I made my best case for not moving. We would no longer have the peach and apricot trees, the garden, our secluded privacy, and worst of all, we would probably have to sell the pony. Plus, we would have way too many neighbors living too close to us. I would miss the feral burros, too. My exploration trips would be not nearly so wild and interesting as those from Trench Mine had been.

But moving was inevitable. I felt like crying at the prospect of losing so much of what I loved so profoundly. Actually, I did cry, but I let no one but Gyp see me doing it.

So before Christmas, we packed up and departed Trench Camp. Blazer, the pony, was sold before we left. We got four hundred dollars which seemed like a really high price. A man from Sonoita wanted him for his daughter. Dad cautioned the fellow that the pony had an ornery streak in him and he often kicked and would buck going downhill, but the man bought him anyway. I missed Blazer, and the feral burros, but not as much as I would have missed our little dog, Gyp, if we had not been able to keep him, why, I would have gone with Gyp, rather than lose him! But Gyp was never in danger of being sold or abandoned by our family.

Now, as I had no pony or burro to carry me around, I rode my bike more. I could use a clothespin to put old playing cards on the front fork which made a sound like a motor and made riding that much more fun. I played with tops, marbles, and yo-yos every day, but I missed the wild country of Trench Camp. I yearned to return to the ways of the mountain men.

At the service station, I got to work for Dad, which was good. I would pump gas and wash the windshields as the tanks were being filled. When things were slow, as they usually were, I cleaned the grease off of Dad's tools and swept the floor and the area around the front of the station. I handled money and made the correct change for customers. And, while in those days a gallon of gas cost twenty-three cents, I got paid twenty-five cents per hour for my work. The money was good, but I never liked being in that kind of business.

Dad hired a local fellow to mind the station during the daytime. This man had a wife and a bunch of kids. The whole Jones family was a scruffy lot and, to me, none of them ever seemed very happy or ambitious. Their house was really dirty and their yard was always extra messy. They were a lowlife bunch in my view.

I remember hearing the man say that he would like to be partners with Dad at the filling station. I relayed that to my parents and told them I didn't like the man or his family. Dad said he thought it might be okay to include them in the business, but Mom disagreed. Luckily Dad did not take the fellow as a partner. Our Dad was always kind to a fault, especially with strangers down on their luck.

Once I was invited to overnight at the Jones's house. I was reluctant to do it, but I figured I had to agree to the invitation. When it was bedtime, I brushed my teeth - a ritual that the other kids stared at, as they were not in the habit - and sat down for a minute in a new style plastic contoured chair. Immediately I felt my butt get wet. When I stood up I got a whiff of human pee. One of the younger kids had peed through his diaper. The pee had sat there getting rancid for who knew how long. I was soaked and thoroughly incensed at this revolting development. I told my parents that I did not want to visit those people's house ever again.

Only about a month after Dad hired the man, he did not show up for work at the station and when Dad went to the house to find out what was going on, he learned that the family had skipped out, telling no one where they were going and owing money to their landlord, the grocery store, and almost everyone else in the little town. Dad had loaned them money, too. We checked the cash register and found it empty. Some of the tools were missing, as well. He estimated that probably a bit over one hundred dollars had been stolen from the cash register, and the tools were worth double that or more. We never heard or saw anything of that family ever again and I sure didn't miss them. If Dad had formally partnered with that loser, maybe we might have had to pay their bills, too.

Dad hired several different men, one at a time, to mind the station, but none stayed on the job very long. A lot of single men were just drifters in those days. They were called bums, and few people had any use for them. Today they're called homeless and get lots of undeserved sympathy, free housing, and welfare.

Not long after New Year's Day Dad decided to only have the station open from about four in the afternoon until nine at night. I went directly from school and usually got to the station before Dad got home from the mine, so I opened things up. I felt pretty grown up about my new responsibilities, but I would rather have been exploring wild places up in the mountains, or even knocking around in the nearby Sonoita River area, to which I often biked.

That spring a man brought in a 1952 Studebaker Commander for routine maintenance. He said it was a good car, but he planned to sell it. It was a four-door sedan and roomier than the 1949 Studebaker Champion that we had. In the course of doing the repairs, Dad thoroughly checked the vehicle out and asked the man what he wanted. The price was right at a few hundred dollars, so we had a "new" car. Dad quickly sold our old car. He said we didn't have to put much money into the new car, so that was a nice side benefit from running the gas station.

Our roomy 4-door Studebaker Commander

My best friend in Patagonia was a kid who lived nearby named Paul Showalter. His Dad had a saddle shop and he did nice leatherwork. He was also a silversmith. Paul and I shot marbles, rode bikes, and hung around together a lot. In 1986 I drove through Patagonia in my 1986 Ford pick-up with Alaska plates, that had my name and Arctic Rivers Guide Service address on the door. As I drove down the road, a police car turned on the siren and set the flashing lights on. I pulled over and it was Paul. He said he wondered if it was me and just wanted to say hello. Paul was the local Marshall and he was the same nice guy he'd been more than thirty years before. In 2014 I spent several days visiting Paul, who had retired from police work. We traveled around on the dirt roads and reminisced.

Me and Paul near the Patagonia service station in 2014.

## Spring 1955 Moving to Tennessee

Before school let out in the spring of 1955, Dad discussed with us all that it looked like the Trench mine operation would close down, so he was looking for another job. I couldn't imagine any place as desirable to me as Trench Camp had been, but I was hopeful that we would move to someplace interesting, like the GroundHog mine at Silver City, New Mexico, or better yet, Whitehorse in the Yukon Territory, maybe Newfoundland or - best of all, someplace - anyplace - in Alaska.

The filling station sold easily and Dad made a small profit from it, but he had put in lots of extra hours of work and improvements on the building. Plus, with the demands of the station, we had less time to go hunting.

When I learned that we would be moving to Tennessee, I was dreadful about what a crowded, overly modernized mess we would find there.

We couldn't take big items or things that we really didn't need, so I had to sell my bicycle and most painful of all, my collection of deer horns and skulls, including that big buck skull that had been killed by a mountain lion. Other kids paid me from ten cents to a quarter for single shed horns. I gave that big buck skull to a good friend, as it was worth far more than mere money.

But I got to keep my BB gun, the old .22 single-shot rifle that I found, and the .22 rifle that Dad had given me.

Most important of all, Gyp, a full-fledged family member, was going with us, of course.

The station had an old single-axel trailer in the back which Dad fixed up to haul our stuff to Tennessee.

The highlight of the trip was the stopover at Grandpa and Grandma's house in El Campo, Texas. I recall a big family potluck and the delicious barbecued chicken, Aunt Erma's potato salad, Aunt Hazel's pumpkin pie and cookies, and, of course, Grandma's chicken and rice goulash, made especially for me, was the highlight of the time.

We made some fishing trips and at a place we called simply, "the River", my Dad caught a Gaspergoo, which is a freshwater drum. That name stuck with me. This fish was a big one at over twelve pounds and made strange grunting noises. A man from across town who claimed to be a cajun gave Grandma a recipe for "goo soup" and it tasted pretty good, but I preferred leftover goulash.

We drove through some beautiful country with mixed forests of hardwood trees, junipers, and cottonwoods as we continued East. We saw cattle and other farm stock in the rural areas, but it seemed to me that most of the time we were threading our way through one big city after another. Big freeways and routes around the larger towns were not in place yet, so we groped our way through the congested areas. Even when we were out of the cities, houses were everywhere. As we traveled I daydreamed and longed for our little barn and corral and the mountains around Trench Camp.

When we got to Knoxville and the house Dad had bought I noticed that some farm fields were not too far off, which gave me hope for the kind of fun activities I liked. Our brick house was a brand new ranch style with three bedrooms. It was part of a new housing development with no grass yet sprouted and no trees in the yard. I had never lived in a new house and was not attracted to this one at all. Of course, we were all tired and Mom's fuse was pretty short. I heard Dad tell Mom that the house cost ten thousand dollars.

"Ten thousand dollars, Max! That's a hundred, hundred dollars!" I heard her say. Having seen relatives lose their farms in the Great Depression, both my parents were scared to death of debt. But now, we were in debt - a lot of debt. Dad talked soothingly to calm Mom down and told her he was sure it would all turn out just fine.

Gyp sensed the tension and just stood there with his head hung down.

Within a couple of weeks of our arrival in Knoxville, Dad told us that he had to go up to Frederick, Maryland to do some exploratory work and he would take the whole family with him for that job which was to last for a month or more.

Any time we stayed in a motel, Mom would carefully check out the beds and chairs, looking for bed bugs which were common back then. I remember more than once, after finding bugs, we would go back to the office and tell the clerk that we would not be staying and why. Mom found bed bugs at two motels on the same night on this trip.

Dad was exploring for uranium, of all things. The job took two months, during which time we made trips to see historically important places like Gettysburg, Bull Run, and other Civil War battlefields. We visited some Revolutionary War sites and, of course, Washington, D.C. Mom told my sister and me that our relatives on her side of the family had engaged in some of those Revolutionary and Civil War battles. Most of her ancestors had been Confederate soldiers, but some had served in the Union Army, too. Dad thought all his ancestors had been with the Northern Army. His people just arrived in the United States from Sweden a few years before the Civil War began.

We rented a house out in the woodland a few miles from town. A farm pond was nearby and I had permission to fish in it. One evening, using a homemade stick pole and earthworms for bait, I caught a largemouth bass from the pond. Weighing more than five pounds, it was the biggest fish I had ever caught. The owner just happened to come by as I walked to the house with the fish and he got angry when he saw it. He had previously told me it was okay to fish in his pond and never mentioned anything about the size of fish I took from it. Dad told me that I'd better not fish there anymore.

There was a lake in downtown Frederick where kids fished and we tried it once, but my sister fell in and I grabbed her by the collar and pulled her out. I was treated like a real hero by strangers who saw the incident as well as my folks, but I figured Pat could have thrashed her way to safety without my help. Anyway, I enjoyed the accolades and fuss.

The summer turned out to be interesting, considering all. When we got back to Tennessee I got a job delivering newspapers and spent my free time kicking around in the farm fields. Old flint chips and Indian arrowheads were easier to find there than they had been in Arizona. The ones I found in Tennessee were broader, heavier, and different in appearance than those from Arizona and New Mexico. Due to the abundance of arrowheads, I reckoned there must have been a lot more Indians in this area than the barren deserts of Arizona and New Mexico.

## FALL, 1954, 7TH GRADE

My sister and I rode a bus to school. It took longer than the ride from Trench Camp to Patagonia and it passed through congested traffic, but there was no alternative. My sister had to ride the bus, no matter her age. I have few memories of that fall, other than my recollection that, thankfully, Dad was soon transferred to northern New Mexico.

We were changing residences more often than I liked to change my sox!

The Knoxville area was growing and the house sold immediately for a little more than Dad had paid for it, so we were lucky on that issue. Mom was adamant that we would not buy a house again until we were sure we would be in the same place for a long time.

The trip back west was great. We stopped again at Grandpa and Grandma's house but only had time to go fishing once, as Dad's job was waiting. When we left El Campo we had a basket full of fried chicken, potato salad, fresh fruit, cookies, and jars of chicken goulash. I think we did not buy any food until we got to our destination. Mom and Dad took turns at the wheel and drove straight through, so we did not stop at any motels. Pat and I slept and fought in the back seat.

When Pat and I woke up one morning in the back seat with Gyp licking our faces, we were in Prewitt, New Mexico, on Route 66, about midway between Grants and Gallup. The wind was blowing hard and dust filled the air and covered everything. I asked if we had come to the Sahara Desert. I half-way expected to see Arabs riding camels.

We were parked next to some box cars on a railroad siding. Prewitt was just a railroad stop with no stores, no school, and not much of anything but dust, dirt, and the smell of creosote from the railroad ties. We were assigned by the mining company to one of the forty-foot box cars which had been modified to make a very small house, with a cook stove, refrigerator, beds, and so forth. Dad's friend from college, Hugh, the beer drinker, and his new family were quartered in one of the boxcars and assured us that living in Prewitt was really nice. No rent was charged.

Pat and I thought it would be really neat, but Mom didn't much care for the idea of living in an old boxcar. Our dog, Gyp, enthusiastically nosed and sniffed everything, as he did with every new place we went.

Dad soon learned that he would be based there in Prewitt, spending a lot of time out with a helicopter looking for uranium, and living in a tent for a week or more at a time. But he told us, he would be making about one thousand dollars a month, which was more than he had ever earned before. A brand new Studebaker cost less than two thousand dollars. It sounded good - money-wise, but Mom said she did not want to live without Dad in that isolated, desolate place. So Dad found a rental house in Grants, which at least had a school and grocery store, but wasn't a very attractive place either.

Grants was a typical boom town. Lots of people had moved in to take whatever job they could get, but there were never enough jobs for everyone. Ethnic clashes further complicated the situation. The population was mostly Hispanic, referred to simply as Mexicans. Navajo Indians from Gallup and the reservations to the west clashed with the Acoma Indians from the east. We, newcomers, were mostly Caucasian and were derided and picked on by everyone. Gangs were well established in the grade school and some of the boys carried dog chain collars to wrap around their fists for fighting.

It was a rough town.

Like all boys my age, I had been in some minor fist fights, but never anything too serious, before living in Grants.

Pat and I could walk the few blocks to school and our route took us right past the Grants Drug and Confectionary Store, which was only three blocks from our house. On rare occasions, we would stop in for an ice cream soda or a malted milkshake. A pleasant older couple, the Humphries, owned the drug store, and one day, Mr. Humphries offered me a job. I was excited beyond belief! I was going to get to be a soda jerk! My schedule was to walk Pat home after school and then go right to work. I would get in two hours on weekdays and sometimes six hours on Saturdays. The pay was fifty cents an hour. I stocked shelves, tore the front cover off of magazines and comics that had not sold, and dump the rest of the booklet. I could take any discarded magazines and comics home, for free. I was to keep the fountain sparkly clean, the floor swept clean and I often mopped all floor spaces. The windows were to be washed at least once per week. I did other jobs as they came up. So, I didn't have any wild places to explore, but I had work that kept me busy. I aimed to do the periodic jobs without being reminded.

And I still had dreams of adventures for which I saved up money to use whenever I might put an adventure into action.

On one of Dad's returns from exploring we visited Bluewater Lake not too far away which had pretty good fishing for small rainbow trout and yellow perch. We used the same old metal telescoping poles that we had in Socorro. Single salmon eggs from a little jar were effective bait whether using a bobber or fishing on the bottom with a weight, and we usually caught a fair number of rainbow trout, with occasionally some Crappies as a bonus. I enjoyed that, but it didn't measure up to the saltwater fishing in Texas. Nevertheless, I would have happily fished there every day, if I could.

Soon after getting my job, I encountered ornery jealousy from some of the other kids, especially the ones who had lived there for a while. I was so happy to have that job, I tried to ignore the taunts and mean comments that frequently came my way.

One Saturday afternoon I was walking on the sidewalk downtown just in front of Dad and Hugh when I saw two of the toughest eighth-grade bullies coming our way. These guys, the Gomez brothers, were Mexicans who had most of the entire grade school intimidated. They were two years older than most of us. As they approached, they separated and when they got next to me on either side, they bumped me hard, then laughed and went on. I couldn't stand to be done that way, especially not in front of my Dad, so I turned back and kicked one from behind - right in the crotch. The kid dropped to the concrete and when his brother turned to see what was happening, I hit him in the mouth as hard as I could swing. He was so surprised he just backed up a step and stood there, so I hit him again. Then both those punks ran down the street.

After I drop-kicked the first one, I heard Dad say "Stop", but Hugh in a louder voice said, "Max, let him go, he's doing all right.»

I was so angry that I had to bite my lip to keep from shedding tears, but I felt really good about how it turned out. The knuckles of my right hand were cut, no doubt from the second kid's teeth, so Mom swabbed my cuts with merthiolate ( I called it "witches spit") when we got home. Those brothers were poisonous I figured, so I asked her to swab me twice.

Hugh joined us for dinner and some of Mom's pie. He told Dad that in a rough town like Grants, a young boy was bound to get into fistfights and I had done a good job with those two punks who were older, bigger, and more experienced than me. My Dad knew all that, but I thought it was good that his buddy mentioned it anyway. Growing up in rural Iowa had been genteel compared with coming of age in a New Mexico boom town.

Word of me and the Gomez brothers got around, as it always does in school. I had an Indian friend from the Acoma Pueblo named Leonard who told me we should fight together if the Mexicans bothered us, but we never did have the need .. or opportunity.

Later on that winter, Leonard got accidentally shot in the face, but the pistol was a .22 caliber. The bullet just went in his cheek and out by his ear. I admired his toughness.

But I was soon to be tested again.

The kid with the reputation of being the toughest in school - named Eber - was three or four years older than the rest of the seventh-grade kids because he had failed and been held back so many times. Eber, at sixteen years of age, looked way different from us twelve-year-olds and was rumored to have already been in Reform School. All the kids were scared of Eber. I guess I was scared, too. He was supposedly half Choctaw Indian and half white, which may explain his different looks and mean nature, but it was more apt to be due to a bad home life, Mom told me.

One Friday afternoon while in the classroom, the teacher had been calling on me often and she praised my responses. Then I noticed that Eber kept glaring at me. He pulled out his dog collar chain, wrapped it around his fist, and made sure I saw it. It was clearly a threat. I was not going to just take his threats without my best efforts to fight him .... and win.

I dreaded having to fight Eber, given his looks, size, and his reputation but figured that sooner or later, a fight would have to come.

Soon after, on the way home from school, I saw Eber with a fresh, full, Dairy Queen milkshake in his hand and decided to confront him.

If I had just bought a milkshake, I sure wouldn't want to risk spilling it over some dumb fight. I counted on him being at least that smart.

"Okay, Eber, it's now or never," I told him.

Well, to my unbelieving horror, Eber just threw his milkshake down and lit into me. Wow, was he strong! He was landing his fists on my head right and left and I was seeing stars with every punch. It was a good thing he wasn't wearing that chain on his fist or I would have been cut to pieces! I had to stop the pounding, so I got in close and grabbed him. His body felt like it was as hard as steel! As we struggled we knocked over a glass telephone booth and both went down with it into the broken glass. Both of us got cut, but Eber, it seemed, was impervious to everything but his project of reducing me to bloody mush and he was well on the way to doing just that. Even rolling around in the dirt and glass I was still getting clobbered faster than I could think.

The telephone booth was mostly glass.

Then, thank goodness - and lucky for me - a police car pulled up. Two uniformed officers separated us and threw us in the back seat. One cop sat between us. We were taken to the police station where we were told to stand at the front desk. A cop stood between us, as Eber seemed like a wild animal, seething with anger and hatred. After writing our names down, the man behind the desk sent Eber straight to a cell - apparently, the cops knew him. The desk sergeant asked me where I lived and what my telephone number was, and then he called my Mom.

Mom came to get me with my sister in tow and the policeman who drove the patrol car told her that she should take me to work because he knew the Humphries would be needing me and I made a good ice cream soda.

Only then did I recognize that cop as a frequent customer at the drugstore.

My face was a mess with a big gash over my left eye, I had cuts on my hands and Mom was pretty upset, but rattled or not, she took me to the drug store. The Humphries doctored me up while Mom was still there and told her that their two boys had been in lots of fistfights in that town, too.

There was nothing to worry about. A young man just had to fight, sometimes, they said. Mom said she would come to get me after work, but Mr. Humphries told her that he would take me home, at least for that day. Before Mom departed, Mrs. Humphries had made a big hot fudge sundae for both Mom and Pat and as she handed them to Mom, she said they were on the house. She gave me one too.

The news of the big fight spread quickly through that dusty little town. It was my second pugilistic incident that month. Several people came in that afternoon to hear the story, which Mr. Humphries was happy to recount, as I scooped ice cream and served the counter, which had more customers than usual that afternoon

As I worked my face felt hot and the swelling around my left eye was starting to obstruct my vision. But, even though I had received the worst beating in my life, I felt like I had won, somehow.

I was worried that I would have to, at least partially, pay for the broken phone booth, but no mention was ever made of it.

When Mr. Humphries dropped me off at home, he handed me a container of ice cream. I never worked for nicer people than the Humphries. So, whether I liked it or not, my personal defense fist-fighting career was fully launched.

It seemed that I healed up in no time and after the big fight with Eber, nobody deliberately provoked or messed with me.

Suddenly I had a lot of new buddies, especially among other newcomer white kids. The white kids were most often the subject of abuse, derision, and attempted intimidation by the local gangs. And whites were always outnumbered, so by the spread of the stories of my two bouts, it seemed I was propelled into some sort of unelected, unexpected, leadership role.

Prejudice was mentioned often, even back in those days. Negroes, Mexicans, and Indians were most often spoken of as being the downtrodden victims of prejudice, but I saw that primarily whites were being discriminated against, especially in school. Shortage of textbooks was common and when, as usual, there weren't enough to go around it was the white kids who went without books far more often than the kids of other races or cultures. Teachers sometimes defended shorting the white kids on the basis that they were not of the "downtrodden" class and usually did better in school anyway. I didn't agree with that practice as I was one of those who were often not given a textbook. I was never a willing martyr or sacrificial lamb.

But despite my sudden popularity, I was never very gregarious and I did not care for group or gang status, so I went about my own personal business as usual. I was basically a loner. I figured everyone had to fight their own battles, but I did step in on a few occasions when I personally witnessed bullying. And more than once I kept an ornery white boy from picking on a smaller Mexican or Indian kid.

Deserved or not, I had gained a reputation. If I was going to be known for something, I wanted it to be for doing good. I did a lot of introspective deliberation on my new status and life in general.

It seemed to me that rain, wind, and snow came down the same on everyone, but when people got mixed into the scene, iniquities and injustices were often introduced. I preferred natural things, out in the wilds, and as devoid of human contamination and interference as possible.

The lyrics, "Give me land, lots of land, under starry skies above, Don't fence me in," served as a sort of philosophical guide to me. I always preferred hunting and fishing to social activities. Carnival rides were fun, but I saw them as synthetic, hollow entertainment, and not of real importance. I could do without them and usually did, saving my money for more important things like .22 ammunition or fish hooks.

As I gained experience and age I believed that children should be lovingly trained and firmly corrected, but I had little sympathy for older kids and adults who made lazy or foolish decisions. To my mind, most drunks, ornery, and impoverished people were in their unenviable situations due to their own faults, and laziness. Most often I saw a self-indulgent lack of deferring gratification as the cause of human misery and financial troubles. I still hold to those beliefs.

And Eber was no longer seen in school. We heard that he had been returned to Reform School. He was not missed.

Acoma Pueblo, the "Sky City"

Leonard from Acoma was my best buddy. We liked and respected each other. I got invited to his Pueblo for a weekend and Mom gave her approval. I liked being with those real Indians in their own village.

Acoma Pueblo was a collection of adjoined adobe houses built atop a mesa that rose above the grass and juniper country below. It had been there for hundreds of years. It reminded me of pictures I had seen of old-time fortresses or European castles. We had to walk up the only winding road that led in and out. The Acoma Indians called it their "Sky City." The houses were clean and neat and I enjoyed my weekend there. People used simply built pole ladders to go to and from the second-story houses. Leonard's Grandpa told us stories and indulged us with treats of dried corn fixings and meat. He referred to us as "young men" and young "warriors", which I enjoyed.

Those Acoma people were not at all like the drunken Indians that frequented Grants. Many of the town drunks were Navajos, but any drunk Indian was referred to as a "drunk Nauvie." Making stereotypes is part of human nature, I guess, and inaccuracies are inevitable, but far too common.

National Prohibition was the law of the land from 1920 until it was repealed by the Twenty-first Amendment in 1933. But by federal law, sale of alcohol to Native Americans (Indians, essentially) was illegal from 1832 until 1953. By the time we arrived in the "Indian Country" of northern New Mexico, the Indians were two years into freely exercising their rights to buy and consume booze. And many of them did not handle that freedom well.

Our rental house in Grants, next to the brushy area where the drunk Indians hung out on weekends.

Across the alley from our rented house was a large warehouse and an adjacent empty lot that was overgrown with tall, dense weeds and bushes. Often, especially on Saturday nights, a bunch of Indians would gather on that lot and sometimes they got pretty noisy with their drinking. If they got a small fire going, the police would soon come by to put out the blaze, sometimes hauling some of the celebrants off to jail, so the partying Indians learned to do without the fire.

The squaws reminded me of walking umbrellas with a woman's head on top. We were told they looked so because they wore several skirts, one on top of the other. That rumor was confirmed when we saw some squaws across the alley from us removing a soiled outer skirt, revealing a cleaner-looking one just underneath as they got ready for the big party. We never saw them carrying dirty skirts, so we assumed that they slipped them back on under the outer, cleaner skirt, for the sake of appearances, I reckon.

Our rented house had a small enclosed front porch with a heavy door secured by a locking knob and a heavy deadbolt on the inside. Once inside the porch room, another locking knob and deadbolt secured the door to the interior of the house. The front yard was open to the street, but a high fence made of old railroad ties circled the big backyard. My little sister and our dog, Gyp, were forbidden from going outside the fenced yard. The back door was as heavy as the front doors and secured in a similar fashion. The landlord told us that since it had become legal for Indians to buy liquor, he had installed extra security and deadbolts on all his buildings.

Mom would go on full alert when she heard the savages whooping it up so close to our house. One night she woke me up to tell me that some drunk was trying to get in the front door. He had already broken the outside door and was on the porch, banging on the inside door. I woke up and wondered why so much noise had not aroused me. That door was stout, but he was hitting it hard with a club of some sort. Mom had a pot of water on the stove, heating up. She said she would throw the water and scald the drunk if he got in, but just in case, I should sit down on the big chair across the room from the door with Dad's double-barreled shotgun and shoot the intruder in the middle of his body, if she yelled for me to do so.

As I dropped the two shells in the barrels I was sure hoping that the guy did not get inside. I was scared and trying not to show my fear. But I was resolved to protect my family.

Mom tried to call the police, but the phone line that entered via the porch was apparently torn loose, so we just sat for a while with the racket going on at the door. The pan of water was soon boiling and we were both nervous, but ready. I think my little sister, Pat, slept through all the commotion.

Finally, Gyp somehow nosed the bedroom door open, (Mom had shut him in there with Pat) and ran barking at the noise on the porch. After a few minutes of the little dog's threatening tirade, the drunk quit his fuss and stumbled outside. We watched from the window, me with the shotgun still in hand. As he crossed the dirt street he fell down and just lay where he fell, right in the middle of the road.

Mom and I stayed in the living room for the night. I dozed off with Gyp on my lap, but I doubt Mom ever slept that miserable night. Sunday morning, the street was clear and we saw no one in the vacant lot. All the revelers were gone. Mom reminded me to take the shells out of the shotgun.

About noon, Mom loaded Pat, Gyp, and me into the car and drove to the police station to report the disturbance. The policeman wrote down some information, then we went home.

That afternoon, being Sunday or not, a telephone repairman came by, and soon our phone rang. Shortly thereafter the police came to see if the line was working again.

For Easter that year Mom and Dad had bought us a little blue chicken. We loved the tiny bird and Gyp seemed to, also. "Blue" as we called him, grew up fast and soon he was a proud rooster. Due to his pooping, he had to spend the nights on the back porch, but he roamed around the house on weekends. Dad poured a little beer in a saucer, Blue drank some and sometimes would walk around with one wing on the ground, awkwardly trying to crow like a big rooster. We all enjoyed Blue.

The most popular soft drink in those days was Coca-Cola. Then Pepsi-cola came along. Other soft drinks, or "pop" (soda) brands were also available, but the colas seemed to sell the best. I discovered Royal Crown Cola, which tasted about the same as the others, to me, but it had the added attraction of costing less. One Sunday afternoon I had just read the latest edition of Prince Valiant in the Sunday Comics section and was planning to have a big RC, but became distracted by music on the radio. I began following the beat with my pocket knife on the unopened RC bottle. Suddenly, the bottle exploded. It made a real mess in the living room and a fragment of that glass grenade hit me in the thumb knuckle of my right hand. I was bleeding profusely, so Mom took me to see the local doctor, whose office was in part of his house. He was disgruntled to be disturbed and had obviously been drinking. When Mom got a whiff of his boozy breath, and watched him clumsily probe around in my thumb wound, she said she would take care of it herself. The doctor said he was nearly finished and placed one black silk stitch to close the gash. My thumb was a long time healing and the base knuckle joint never had the normal range of motion. In 1958 the knuckle was especially sore one day, so I began to squeeze on it, and out popped a sliver of RC cola bottle glass. The drunk doctor in Grants had missed it and it took over three years to work its way out. I sure noticed a difference, and I regained the full range of motion in my thumb when the glass shard was gone.

Other than the Humphries and my job at the drug store, I didn't like living in Grants, New Mexico much at all.

## Late Fall 1955 - we move back to Arizona

That winter, Dad told us that he had a job offer in Arizona. A new mine was being developed at a massive, low grade copper deposit that was projected to last for decades. If he took the job we would live in a new company rental house and Dad would do shift work, but basically, he would be home with the family. And, best of all, we probably would not need to move again for a long time. I figured that would be great if the country was nice.

Dad and I made the first trip to the new townsite. We drove over the Continental Divide, then through some really hungry-looking, desolate high desert to Holbrook, Arizona. I thought this country was almost as undesirable as Socorro, New Mexico had been - maybe even worse, because it had no river. By the time we reached Show

Low, the country was pretty attractive. We headed southerly along the western border of the White Mountain Apache Reservation which was a beautiful mountainous country. We drove into Globe, then south through some good-looking country which petered out before we got to Winkleman. The Gila River flowed through that old mining town, but even a year-round river couldn't make it look good to me. Darn, why couldn't the mine be located a little way south of Show Low, I wondered. We came to Dudleyville, which was appropriately named. Then Mammoth which was set in the bottom of a dry valley with the trickling San Pedro River, sometimes running in places, but most of the time it was completely dry. At last, we arrived in San Manuel. To me, it looked like scorched earth, with a lot of jumping cholla cactus as trimming. The town was laid out very nicely. All the cookie-cutter houses were newly constructed, and made of concrete blocks. The shopping mall was brand new and made of the same material. I was turned off by the new, look-alike buildings and the straight, paved streets. I was sure I was hearing the "call of the mild", and it repelled me.

The surrounding country was an unattractive desert, loaded with predominantly cholla cactus - the jumping variety - with a few mesquite and palo verde trees and other varieties (or perversions) of cacti - prickly pear and many others, mixed in. My dream of a return to a place like Trench Camp was dashed.

My Dad decided to sign up and we were offered a choice of houses. We wound up with a three-bedroom ranch-style house, at 235 McNabb Street. It was larger than the brick home in Tennessee. And the monthly rent was really low - about thirty dollars a month, as I recall. At least the house was within easy walking distance of the undeveloped desert and I saw plenty of cottontail rabbits in the cholla patches, so that was some consolation for me.

Dad and I traveled back to Grants, I said good-bye to my buddy, Leonard, and a few others then I gave big hugs to the Humphries. We loaded the car and trailer, got Mom and my sister comfortable, and we departed for our new home in southern Arizona.

As the whole family was driving to the new town, we stopped at a small restaurant and ordered a "pizza pie". It was the first time we had ever even heard of pizza. It was greasy and really tasty, but I was hungry and chomped into my piece too soon. The roof of my mouth was burned by the hot cheese, and when I tried to spit it into my hand, my lower lip got burned, too. But I liked the taste.

235 McNabb Street in San Manuel, Arizona

San Manuel was another mining boom town. The school was extremely crowded. At first, there were sixty, then more than eighty kids in my seventh-grade classroom. Of course, there were not enough textbooks to go around. The new kids signed up for books which were to be issued when available based on when kids had arrived. But that policy was not followed. I never did get any textbooks that first year as the teachers passed them out preferentially to "minority" students, especially those that spoke with a Mexican accent. It was the same unofficial system of preference as the one in Grants. That prejudice just galled the heck out of me, and still does!

Water pistols were popular that spring and the local Five and Dime store had some. I got one and during the lunch hour one day, I was squirting two giggling girls when my seventh-grade homeroom teacher, six foot eight inch tall Tom Cash, came up behind and slapped me on the right side of my head. He was a six-foot, eight-inch tall former college basketball player and the force of his slap knocked me off my feet. He grabbed me by my shirt, stood me up, shook me off, and told me I was to get three swats at his desk. I really couldn't hear my sentencing as my ear was ringing. My right ear rang for more than a day from that blindside slap. When it finally quit ringing I was glad that I was no longer deaf.

My disciplinary swats were delivered when school resumed at one o'clock. I took the punishment without so much as a grimace, as was expected of boys my age. But I could barely hear the cracking of the paddle on my butt as my ear was still ringing. I never did forgive that teacher for the slap on the ear. He, no doubt was stressed with so many students in such a crowded room, but his action was unconscionable. Adults, especially those in positions of responsibility and power, should have better control of their temper, I figured.

When I got home, Mom noticed that my face was red and had to hear the story. When Dad saw my face and got the facts, he went to the school to tell the teacher that he had better never slap me again. The swats were okay, but slapping, especially on the head was not going to be tolerated. Pop was really angry, I seldom saw him get so torqued at any stranger.

Prior to the slap I had sensed that the teacher did not like me. His lack of affinity for me didn't change, but after Dad talked to him, he never slapped me again. I did my best to show my disdain for the jerk.

Also, I learned to be more cautious when squirting or teasing girls. Innocent fun can lead to problems.

The kids in this school were friendly enough. Most of us were newcomers and we all had at least that much in common. I was not aware of any gangs or such in San Manuel.

## San Manuel

Most of the company houses did not have good grass lawns yet, but the water was plentiful and not metered, so lawns were coming in. I saw this as an opportunity to make some good money. I wanted to replace the job I had left in Grants - any kind of work would do as far as I was concerned, but San Manuel did not have a good old-fashioned soda fountain.

Initially, I bought an old used push mower - like Grandpa used in Texas. It cost seven dollars. At a flat rate of seventy-five cents per lawn with an average of one to two hours to mow and trim one, I was making decent money by doing four or five yards per day on weekends. Soon, I began to consider the benefits of using a gas mower and discussed it with Dad. He agreed that a power mower would be a good business decision. He said he would help me look for one.

San Manuel was built on the west side of a broad valley. The higher end of the town was connected by paved streets to the lower part of the community. If I pushed my mower up a street on one side, soliciting lawn work, then came down the other side offering the same service, normally I would get several jobs each way. The trip back home was downhill which was a real plus. After a full day in the hot dry conditions, I appreciated the downhill leg home. If I returned in two weeks or so the lawns were ready to be cut again. Few other kids were interested in mowing lawns, even their own, so there was enough work to keep me busy full-time - during after-school hours and on Saturdays.

The few other kids who were doing a little lawn cutting were not consistent in their work. Most charged a dollar and a half for cutting and trimming with an extra dollar for large corner lots and most of them did not do a neat job with the trimming. I knew I could make plenty of money by charging a straight dollar and a quarter per lawn, corner lots included. A haircut cost the same and takes lots less time and effort to do.

There were several hundred houses in town, virtually everybody had a good job, and it seemed that most of the residents did not care to cut their lawns. So, about the time school was letting out for the summer, Dad and I went to Tucson and I bought a used single-cylinder gas-powered lawn mower for about sixty dollars, and a pair of hand-operated trimmers. Like with milking cows, the hand-squeezed trimmers made my forearms stronger and my muscle definition more noticeable, which I liked.

On the first day, I got eight jobs, earned ten dollars, and had only gone half of a block. I was in business, big time! I soon appreciated how a host of unpredictable factors could and usually did, make my day less than perfect. So, I accepted that imperfections were to be expected and just needed to be accommodated.

I became acquainted with Murphy's Law.

Lawn and yard work wasn't nearly as much fun as dealing with livestock or even being a soda jerk, plus there were no free comics and magazines, but some people, mainly women and older men, would give me a glass of iced tea and little snacks. On rare occasions, I would be given a money tip, but I never expected any. And, I was getting to know just about everybody in town.

Money was never plentiful in our family and I was parsimonious with mine. After all, I had some big items to save up for. Soon I found a nice used CCM boy's bicycle with an intact chain guard for fifteen dollars. I wanted a Schwinn but this would do fine, so I splurged on that. I wanted a chain guard as I had seen too many kids get their pant cuffs caught and wound up in the chain sprocket, sometimes causing awful wrecks. I had enough wrecks without the extra risk of having no chain guard. A guy could make pant leg clips with spring-loaded clothespins, but it would be easy to lose them and they were not as dependable as a regular chair guard.

Gambel Quail and Mourning Doves were abundant, so a shotgun was high on my list of needed items. In the local newspaper, the San Manuel Miner, I saw a classified advertisement for a 16-gage bolt action shotgun. It was listed at an address on my next day's lawn mowing route, so I stopped by to ask about the gun. The older gentleman who came to the door showed me the gun. It had a variable choke on the end of the barrel and the stock was beautifully carved, showing a quail in flight. I told the man that I would take it, but he said I would have to bring my Dad by to approve the sale. When Dad went back with me that evening the man said he would trade the gun to me for lawn work. I was pretty fast with everyday math and I said that would be twenty mowings. I figured only about two mowings per month would be necessary on his lawn which was not very lush. I didn't want to wait for nearly a year for that gun, so I said maybe I should just pay him for it, as I had the money saved up.

The guy must have been reading my mind. He said, "Young man, you can take the gun now, but we've got to shake hands on the deal and you can mow my lawn tomorrow and every two weeks or so until you've paid it off". He told me to just go ahead and mow even if he wasn't home and keep track of how many times I had done it, then after twenty mowings, he would have to start paying me, if he liked my work. He handed me two boxes of number seven and a half shot, which he said worked well on dove and quail. He said I could set the choke full for long shots or open cylinder for close-ups, but it was probably best to leave it somewhere in between the two settings.

He and Dad began talking. He said he was a "contract miner" and got paid according to what he produced, unlike the ordinary day-wage miners. Apparently, he made a lot more money that way and he wasn't afraid to spend it.

Eventually, Dad became a contract miner and made more take-home pay that way than he had earned as a salaried engineer, using his college degree.

My savings account was growing as I made weekly bank deposits. We had some used factory-made furniture and Dad was building more pieces as well. He bought a Craftsman table saw which allowed him to produce furniture faster. He used cholla cactus skeletons to make some unique lamps and shelving. Occasionally we would acquire another piece when someone was moving, but we did not buy new furniture. It was just too costly. Our kitchen table and chairs were really old and ratty, so when I had fifty dollars saved up I withdrew it from the bank and gave it to Mom, so she could pick out a new kitchen set. She nearly cried when I handed her the cash. We all drove to Tucson to look at tables and chairs and she found a brand new set with a Formica tabletop at a discount store for forty dollars. She gave me back the ten dollars. I handed it right back to her and said I would buy dinner. McDonald's burgers were available on our way home, so that's where we had our supper. Burgers cost seventeen cents apiece back then, so we all ate two burgers, had a milkshake and still had money left over for a watermelon to take home. And Mom still had some change from my ten bucks to give back to me. It was a great day.

I needed a bigger rifle for deer hunting and sure enough, the San Manuel Miner had an ad for a Winchester lever action Model 94. It was a .32 Special. I had planned on a 30/30, but the owner of this brand new-looking carbine was asking only thirty-two dollars, so I bought it. He threw in nearly two full boxes of shells and a Lee Loader. I could load my own bullets for about one-fifth the cost of a box of factory shells. I was elated at that prospect!

Miners and their families would come and go, so I watched for signs of people moving and began accumulating camping items that I thought I would need. I got a nearly new Trapper Nelson pack board for a dollar, an inflatable sleeping mattress, a small camping stove, and other useful pieces at low cost. All the things I found cost way less than the store prices, and most were in nearly new condition.

## Biking Around

So, I was set up pretty well soon after we got moved in at San Manuel. I kept at the lawn work and used that bicycle to explore the area. After church one Sunday two of my school friends, Leon and Dick, and I packed lunches and rode our bikes down the hill to the San Pedro River, which was actually more of a creek than a river, but it was the only waterway in that immense valley. Right away, we found an old gravel borrow pit that was full of clean-looking water. The sides were steep, but we found a safe way to get down to the water. On that hot, sunny day, a swim was called for.

None of us had anticipated a swim and no one else was around, so we just peeled off our clothes and skinny-dipped.

The hole was deep, the water was cool and we were having a fine time swimming until Leon yelled "SHARK!" We all churned the water in our mad dash to the safety of the bank.

I noticed frogs sitting on the shoreline mud and one painted turtle sunning itself. The shark had apparently morphed into a common amphibian. We didn't spend time trying to catch any, but a catching trip was definitely in our future. I had a three-prong, barbed frog gig - a vital piece of survival equipment, that I'd kept from our time in Tennessee.

As we were lying in the sun to dry off, I found a piece of broken Indian pottery, some flint chips, and a small arrowhead. We all began scratching around on a rounded hill overlooking the river. There were lots of shards of pottery, but we found no more arrowheads that afternoon. We named the place Indian Hill and vowed to return to thoroughly investigate the ancient village site.

The road back to town was steep and all uphill, so we pushed our bikes most of the way. After more than an hour, we could see the first houses. It had been a great day for me in this area so close to our new home. We planned to revisit our swimming hole and Indian Hill as soon as we could. This place couldn't hold a candle to Trench Camp, but it had some good features and I planned to make the best of what I found.

The two smelter smokestacks with the Galiuro Mountains in the background.

The San Manuel skyline was punctuated by two giant smokestacks that expelled the gasses and other waste effluvia from the smelter. Often, due to temperature inversions or whatever, the thick, sulfur-laden smoke would settle in the valley and hang in there for days. It was pretty nasty stuff. We could not only smell the smoke - we could taste it, too. So far as I know, prolonged inhalation of that horrible sulfur smoke did not cause severe health problems.

When the sulfur smoke wasn't occluding our visibility, the barren Galiuro Mountains beckoned from across the valley to the east. Up the slope to the west rose the pine-covered Catalina Mountains. The rust-colored cliffs of the Galiuros were a magical attraction for me, but the distance was far and the road was bad, so most times we would make our single day forays into the oak and pine-covered Catalinas. One nice aspect of our bicycle explorations to the West was that we had a downhill route most of the way back home.

## Spelunkers

One Sunday in the fall, when the lawn mowing had slowed down, my two friends, Dick and Leon, and I loaded our lunches and extra water into our Trapper Nelson backpacks which we usually carried on long bicycle journeys. This was to be a long trip up the road into the Catalinas, so we started plenty early.

A few dusty miles from town we encountered a small rattlesnake crossing the road, so, of course, we stopped, killed it, and drew grass straws for who was to keep the rattle. I was not lucky that time. I would have skinned it, if I'd won.

Peppersauce Creek ran clear and pretty year-'round, but considering the local history of mining and the long-time presence of cattle, we were averse to drinking its untreated water, unless we treated it with a Halazone tablet, so we normally carried plenty of the pills and a couple of canteens for each traveler.

Up the hill and around a bend from the Creek we located Peppersauce Cave. The entrance was on the side of a hill amidst some oaks, juniper trees, ocotillo, and Spanish dagger. A large rock had fallen in front, concealing the mouth of the cave from view until one was standing very close. As other kids had told us of the cave and its location, we couldn't claim the right of discovery, but we still felt like real explorers.

This cave was said to have been discovered in 1951, just around four years before our visit. We young fellows had all been cautioned by parents, teachers, and mine executives to not fool around in any caves or mine shafts, but we figured that because this was a natural cave, it should be safe enough. A person can rationalize almost anything that he wants to bad enough, I reckon. This cave sure looked a lot less spooky than the old wooden culverts I'd helped explore at the Trench Mine site.

We stashed our bikes in some manzanita brush, checked our flashlights, and started into the cave.

The cave entrance.

We crouched down and entered one in front of the other, all with flashlights in hand. It was necessary to go on our hands and knees for a short distance. Soon we had to squeeze our bodies, standing on our feet, through a narrow vertical gap in the rock, and shortly thereafter we were forced to get on our bellies and slither through another, even tighter spot. It was good that we had flashlights and did not encounter snakes or big spiders. Those were spooky passages. We came to a much larger chamber with plenty of headroom. This was a nice echo chamber. Our adventure was becoming very interesting and fun! I made some sounds to test the echoes, then I let out a yodel, but my partners told me to quit, as it was getting on their nerves. I think they were spooked, but maybe it was my tone. I never was a good singer, anyway.

As we proceeded I wondered if we would encounter a skunk - I'd been there and done that before and did not relish a repeat performance.

We searched the area carefully for snakes, as there were lots of serpents in the surrounding desert and this sure looked like an ideal place for a snake den. But we found only rocks on the dusty floor. Another potential danger was bats, but we saw no sign of any of those hideous little buggers. When we turned our flashlights off, it was eerie, silent, and completely black.

The air was fresh enough to make us wonder if we would come upon another entry or maybe see some light coming through the top, but we found no sign of either. After what seemed like a long time of slow, cautious progress, we came to a very deep hole. Our flashlights were not strong enough to show the bottom. We dislodged some rocks to throw into the abyss. Judging from the time the rocks left our hands until we heard them impact below, we knew that hole was dangerously deep.

If we fell in, we discussed the horror of someone in the future tumbling down, to find our bare skeletons lying at the bottom. I reminded my companions that no one knew where we were, but if we fell in, eventually our bikes would be discovered and rescue would be attempted, maybe even before we died from starvation, fright, or whatever else might get us. I became aware of echoes from our hushed conversation, so I gave a shout. This time my whoop caused some extremely unnerving echoes. We mutually agreed to not tempt any lurking evil spirits and that it was time to vacate the cave.

As we groped our way toward the entrance, the return route seemed right, but after what seemed like a prolonged time we came to a dead end.

We were lost in the strange labyrinth! We were self-buried in the belly of the mountain.

Leon blurted out that he was scared all along that we would get lost in there and we had left our lunches with the bikes, so we might starve. I felt a pang of panic, too, but told my companions that we had to carefully figure our way out of there. We should turn around and go back the way from which we had just come and watch for other routes - and, especially, watch that we did not fall into any holes. The floor of the cave was dusty which held our tracks, but it might have been traversed by the boots of others who probed its forever-dark recesses before our attempt. With no wind or rain, the tracks lasted forever in the cave. But, still, the signs on the floor ought to reveal the way out, or so I reasoned ... and hoped.

After a few minutes - which seemed like "half of forever" - we could find no alternate route. We seemed to be at another dead end. We needed to stand in place, fight the panic, inspect our surroundings, and think. I had new batteries in my flashlight, but my friends' hand-held lights were losing their brightness, so I told them to turn theirs off to save the batteries. We all had a drink of water from our canteens. I was getting scared but didn't want my friends to know that. We were all scared and getting more frightened with each exhaled breath. Our situation seemed thoroughly dreadful. I reminded myself that Dad had told me that panic causes people to do dumb things, so we had to fight panic. Scanning around with my light, I saw disturbances in the dust of the floor leading to a small overhang at the far end of the room we were occupying. Just then I remembered that we had to belly crawl once through such a hole to get inside. That was it! Drag marks in the dirt indicated that was, maybe, the tight little passageway from which we had come. Or, was it maybe a similar hole leading deeper into the unknown? Or to a mantrap? There was only one way to find out.

Leon mentioned that if it was not the right hole, we might get even more lost. He was thinking, it seemed, but his voice was quavering at least two octaves higher than normal.

But we had to try. I volunteered to go first and if I got through, I would holler to the others. If it was not possible to get completely through the crawlway, I would just worm my way back out and rejoin my buddies.

Leon said he sure hoped I didn't crawl into a big bunch of snakes or spiders.

He just had to say that! In the dim light, he couldn't see the ornery look I gave him. I didn't need any more spooky scenarios at that point. None of us did.

The tight crawlway went for less than twenty feet. On the other side, I spotted a small piece of chewing gum wrapper. None of us had any gum that day, so it must have been dropped by a previous spelunking idiot. I was never so happy to see litter before. The thought crossed my mind that maybe the gummer had taken the wrong route and might still be in there, but I suppressed mentioning that negative possibility. I yelled for my friends to join me and soon we were negotiating the vertical squeeze slot. From there we groped along for only a few minutes before we saw light from the entrance.

Before we stood in the welcome sunlight we were all devoid of panic and probably would not have admitted to having been scared, even to each other. But, truth be told, we'd all been nearly petrified with fear.

Leon, having recovered his composure and self-esteem along with his normal voice, mentioned that before we go in again, we must get a couple of rolls of kite string to mark our way. That was brave of him .... or was he making up for his recent scare? I hadn't yet even entertained a thought of a return visit to the cave. But now, I figured we had to have another go at it.

With hunger now dominating our other sensations, we wasted no time getting to our bikes and lunches. It was well past mid-afternoon, so we must have spent close to three hours in that dark cave. I had a special treat - a can of sardines - which I opened and shared with the other guys. As Leon hesitated before popping one of the little fish into his mouth, I asked if they had noticed the human skull back at the first dead end. Leon dropped the sardine into the dirt. Both my comrades glared at me.

"Aw, I was only kidding, but it could have happened," I offered after a pause. Leon wiped the dirt off of his sardine and ate it.

We all agreed that it would not be a smart thing to tell our families of our trek into the unknown bowels of the mountain. Enlightened and enriched by the experience as we had become, we could prepare for another attempt to plumb the mysteries of the cave, but for sure we would have to bring plenty of extra flashlight batteries, lots of string, and maybe another buddy or two. But nobody that was too fat should be invited, lest they become irretrievably wedged in a tight spot which could lead to our terror, even the death of us all. Yeah, we vowed to properly explore the caverns of Peppersauce. - and to keep our plan secret from everybody but the three of us.

It was something to look forward to.

Of course, none of us even considered wearing protective headgear, knee pads, or special boots. Such safety paraphernalia was not common back in those days.

When we reached Peppersauce Creek on the way home we had consumed all our food and most of our water. It seems being nervous acts like a super appetizer. We still had a long way to go and it was going to be well after dark before we could see the lights of town. We knew that our luck had not deserted us when a rancher came by in his pick-up. We waved, and he stopped to offer us a ride to the Oracle Road turn-off. We happily loaded our bikes and packs in the bed of his truck. It was mostly downhill biking from that junction on home.

On our ride back to town we encountered several coveys of Gambel quail scurrying across the road and Mourning doves were seen in abundance. Just before dark we saw two mule deer does crossing the road ahead of us. I was encouraged by that, as hunting season was just about to open.

Before we finally drug ourselves all the way home after dark we discussed the inevitable questions from parents and others about our activities of the day. We agreed to stick to our plan to omit any mention of Peppersauce Cave.

We made a couple of short forays into the cave after that, bringing girls along on one memorable trip, but we didn't go so deep. The girls kept up a nervous chatter - and kept very close to us. That part was nice.

In 2014 I read that approximately twenty-three thousand people visited Peppersauce Cave annually. It would not have held the attraction for me if it had been so well visited back in 1955. Plus so many visitors probably brought about requirements for safety measures, etc.

## FIRST DEER

That fall after school started the local druggist offered me a job. For fifty cents an hour, I could clean the toilets, mop the floors, and wash the windows of his store. If I proved up, I might get work stocking shelves and even dealing with customers at the counter, making change, and so forth. Those jobs would pay a little better hourly wage, too - twenty-five cents more! I was making way more than that mowing lawns, even in the "off" season, but I took the job. Who knows, maybe a grass blight would hit and I'be be out of work. It's always good to have one's eggs in more than one basket.

This drugstore was not like the old-fashioned one in Grants. This one had no soda fountain and did not make sundaes. This modern store wasn't nearly as much fun as the Humphries' drugstore in Grants had been, but I was happy to work any place I could get a job.

As Dad was a newly hired staff member, having been on the job just less than a year, he had little vacation time built up and was low on the seniority totem pole when it came to setting or changing his shifts. He had the day shift and weekends to work when deer season opened, so that meant that we would not be able to hunt on opening day.

The pharmacist, Doug, like most locals, was new to the area, too. When he learned that I liked to hunt, he asked if I could go with him and his friend, Al, on opening day. I think he figured that I knew some good places to go, but he was wrong in that assumption and I made no effort to correct him. Dad went up to the store, visited with the druggist, and gave permission for me to go hunting with him.

This was early in my eighth grade year and I was thirteen years old.

We loaded up the Doug's Chevy station wagon with a big mattress in the back and departed right after school on Friday afternoon. I told him that I liked the Galiuro Mountains, but was only vaguely familiar with them.

We drove down to the dusty San Pedro River road, then turned south toward Reddington. Before finally heading east toward the mountains, Doug stopped to ask a scruffy-looking kid we saw standing near an old set of corrals about the whereabouts of the road that would take us up into the Galiuros. The kid mumbled that he didn't rightly know, but it was maybe one or five miles further. Al said the kid acted like he was from Appalachia or some such place. One or five miles ... who ever heard of such vague directions?

The road was suitable for a four-wheel drive vehicle, not a standard station wagon, nevertheless, Doug plugged along, scraping the undercarriage and rear bumper intermittently until well after dark. He parked for the night on a ridge, still several miles short of the base of the mountains.

None of us had any idea where we were.

The three of us wadded up on the mattress in the back, put our sleeping bags over our bodies, and tried to sleep.

Well before sunup we had a cup of cocoa and a doughnut, stuffed a candy bar in our pockets, strapped on our army surplus canteen belts, and set out walking downhill to the north. From a vantage point a short distance from our ridge we could glass a broad valley that looked pretty desolate to me, but Doug thought we should separate by a hundred yards or so and sit for a while to see what might happen as it got lighter. I was on the west side of our party, the riverside, downhill from the others. A small draw down the hill from me led into the larger valley.

Staring through my Dad's field glasses, as binoculars were often called, I saw some birds - flickers probably - and then two javelinas across the valley, but no deer appeared to inhabit that hungry, cactus, creosote, and palo verde-infested, country.

About a half hour after sunup, I heard some shooting way down the valley to the west of us. The shooting seemed to be getting closer as the minutes passed. Then I saw the deer. A huge buck with a much smaller one was running toward us on our side of the valley. I jacked a round into my barrel, lowered the hammer to make it safe, and hoped they would come close enough for a shot. I practiced aiming through my buckhorn sights at a barrel cactus. I wanted to be ready to throw the gun to my shoulder and quickly get a bead on a deer if an opportunity came my way.

I felt the tension each time the deer would disappear from view in a low spot, but soon they would loom up again. They were maintaining a tack that should put them just below me. When they topped off on the far side of the draw to my left they were still way out of range but coming to me.

Buck fever was upon me. I had never experienced that before. I tried to steady my nerves, but I was trembling. I so wanted to shoot that big buck!

The deer were by then slowed down a bit and I could see their tongues hanging out from the long run. I pulled back the hammer on my carbine and waited behind a small mesquite tree until the bigger buck was coming up the hill to me. He was only about fifty yards away when I squeezed the trigger. I heard the bullet hit him and he went down! It was my first deer!

The smaller buck, a spike, turned back down the small draw and was out of sight in no time. My buck staggered to get up. I shot three more times but missed him with all three shots. As I attempted to jack another round into my barrel the bullet flew off to the side. I probably had jacked the lever an extra stroke to cause that to happen.

In frenzied haste I groped in my pocket for another bullet as the deer struggled down the draw, dragging his hind legs. He never regained his feet.

I pulled out my chapstick and tried to stuff that in the barrel of my carbine. When I realized what I was doing I threw the chapstick down and fished out a real bullet.

By then the buck was about eighty yards away and still headed downhill. I stumbled after him with my gun ready and reloaded to finish him off.

When I was close to getting ready to shoot again, a man and a woman on horses came over the ridge of the draw, jumped off their horses, and started shooting at my deer. Their missed shots were busting rocks only a few yards from my position. Then one of them hit my struggling buck.

The man got busy trying to catch the horses which were spooked and mulling around with their bridle reins dragging on the ground in front of them. The woman scrambled down the slope, nearly falling several times, but got to the buck just after I did.

"That's my deer," she screamed at me.

"Well, I shot it first and it wasn't even on its feet when you shot," I said.

The man came toward us, leading the horses and he was angry. He told me that they had been chasing those deer all morning and the lady was going to have that buck.

All the shooting and commotion had drawn Al to the scene. He had seen part of the action and heard the conversation. He told the horse people that it seemed like since "the kid" had hit the deer first, had it on the ground, and was ready to finish it off before they shot, the deer belonged to him. That made perfect sense to me.

Tensions were high and the man with the horses was getting really loud and profane.

Then we heard a shot below us.

The woman was hustling to get her paper deer tag punched and wrapped around one antler. It was a big four-point buck with heavy antlers. That buck was beautiful, probably the prettiest deer I had ever seen.

Al did some cussing of his own as he told the man and woman what low-life skunks they were to steal a deer from a kid like that. But he didn't offer any more than words.

As for me, I was so sad and angry, I had to fight to keep my tears away. I remembered Dad's admonishing me to never overreact - as I had done with throwing the big rock at the fleeing Mexican that had been dismantling our front porch at Trench Mine.

The man, pot-bellied and rough-looking, barked at the woman to help him load the buck. The two of them got it draped over the saddle on the man's horse, which got spooked by the blood and all the goings on and lunged downhill, nearly getting away. The woman grabbed the reins, handed them to the man, got on her horse, and with that ornery man leading his horse with the deer aboard, they went back down the valley - with my buck.

Boy, I was really downcast at being robbed of my first ever buck - and such a big one, too. I could hardly believe what had happened.

Al was still muttering about how he would find out who that S.O.B. was and spread the word of his cowardly deed. But we never did learn who he was or where he was from.

Feeling completely drained of energy and enthusiasm, I heard Doug holler. He told us to come down as he had killed a deer and needed help. My energy came back, but my spirit was still punctured.

Before going to Doug I went back and retrieved my chapstick and the live bullet I had ejected. I told myself that I would never again carry chapstick in the same pocket as my bullets.

In Doug's yard with Al, me & the spike buck.

Doug told us that he had seen the two bucks coming and heard my shots. He watched the spike buck tear off down the draw, then stop near a big mesquite tree. The buck was standing there, panting, when Doug got within range of his 30:06 and knocked it down.

Neither Doug, Al, nor I had ever gutted a deer, but I had helped Dad do one, so I had a chance to prove my worth. I unsheathed my K-bar and carefully removed the guts without puncturing the stomach or intestine. We saved the heart and liver, leaving the rest of the entrails for the coyotes and foxes.

The big hill we had come down seemed to grow a lot higher as we dragged the gutted deer back toward the car. I had a small piece of rope in my pocket which I tied to the head, and a short piece of stick on the other end for me to grip, which helped a lot, but the men had an awkward trip with one pulling on each front leg. They fell several times. I was thinking that I would learn to cut a deer carcass up and carry it in my Trapper Nelson pack, rather than ever again having to drag one out very far by myself.

We had one spike buck, but the big one was stolen from me.

When we reached the station wagon, we were all worn out. As he devoured his lunch, Doug suggested we just call it a day and head back to town. Neither Al nor I objected. At least we got one deer.

That evening when Doug dropped me by the house he and Al came in and told Dad what had taken place that day. I just stood there silently.

Dad came over, put his hand on my shoulder, and told me that he was proud of the way I had acted in such a really difficult situation.

Later, Dad told me that all my life I would encounter some people who were so small, selfish, and ornery that we could never anticipate how low they would act. It was our duty to remain calm and rational, to not overreact to others.

## Fish of the Desert

My friend, Dick, and I returned to the borrow pit/ swimming hole one Saturday. Leon was invited, but couldn't make it. Dick and I just couldn't put the trip off. We had seen small fish in the San Pedro River, so we each took along a fishing rod, some hooks, and sinkers, just in case. It was too windy and cool to swim, so we poked around the shallow river, finding only some guppy-sized fish. There were no holes or stretches deep enough to bother with regular fishing.

Across the broad, mostly dry, river bed we saw some large green cottonwoods, so we walked over to check the area out. On the other side of a tight five-wire stock fence, we could see a circle of bull rushes. We knew that meant a pond was nearby, so we went through the fence and found a beautiful lake of about two acres in size. We noticed some small disturbances on the water's surface and suddenly a big fish jumped. I recognized it as a bigmouth bass. When I was gathering up hooks and stuff I had put a small River Runt bass plug in my bag (I'd had it since fishing at Kolbe's stock pond years before), so I put it on the line, cast it out near where the fish had jumped and, BANG, I got a strike. I reeled in a large mouth bass of about three pounds!

My excitement was indescribable! We had found a place to fish, and it had some dandy fish in it!

This, I told Dick, was a secret that must be kept just between the two of us. He nodded his head enthusiastically.

A trip to Roosevelt Lake the next summer with my teacher Catfish McClure produced a nice catch of bass. Note my homemade barbells.

In a few minutes, I caught another bass of similar size and then handed my pole to my friend. He made three casts and got a nice bass, too. Some dragonflies were flitting around the pond and we witnessed what appeared to be a much larger bass jump and grab one of the big insects. We were sure there might be some monster bass in that little pond. Our youthful imaginations went wild. Who knew just what might be in that pond? How long had it been there and how long since someone fished it? We'd spent so much time messing around with the minnows in the river, it was already time to push for home. We had no stringer or bag for the fish, so I cut a forked limb from a small bush and used it to hold our catch. The fork kept the fish from slipping off and I tied the fork ends together. Near the spot where we'd hidden our bikes, we found a paper bag. I slipped it over the fish, in case anyone came by. We had to guard our newfound secret. That small pond couldn't stand too much pressure.

Sure enough, when we got within a mile of town a neighbor came by in a pick-up and offered us a ride. I thanked him, but fearing he might see the fish, told him we needed the exercise.

My folks were truly amazed to see the bass. The two fish were enough for us to have a nice fresh fish fry. I could hardly wait to get back to that pond.

## FIRST BIG GAME KILL

The wild pig-like animals common to parts of Texas, Arizona, New Mexico, and points south are commonly referred to as Javalina. More properly they are called Collard Peccary (*Pecari tajacu*). They are not true pigs, but, due to their noses and behavior, most people consider them to be wild hogs and refer to them as such.

In February of 1956, Javalina season was about to open. I was planning to go pig hunting near town when a call came from Patagonia. My old neighbor, Glen, was calling to see if I wanted to go with him and two others to hunt pigs in the Whetstone Mountains which were located about midway between San Manuel and Patagonia. His buddies were both going to college at the University of Arizona in Tucson. Was this a long-term pay-off from my not breaking faith over the skunk in the school ventilation venture? Maybe so, but it was very thoughtful of Glen.

Of course, I wanted to go. Not only would this be a new area, but it would probably include a return to my favorite little town, Patagonia. The plan was set for Dad to drive me to Tucson on Friday, meet Glen, and we would go hunting from there. Oh well, even without going to Patagonia, it still was appealing to me. Dad mentioned that I should avoid temptations, recalling our tryst with the skunk. I assured him that everything would be on the up and up.

The Whetstones are much like other small mountain ranges in southern Arizona. The range looks quite barren from a distance, but where not overgrazed by cattle, the grass can be lush, long and nutritious. Junipers, ocotillo, agaves or century plants, mesquite trees, and various types of cactus dot the foothills. Scattered patches of prickly pear cactus were favored by javelinas, as were the acorns of the Mexican live oak trees found at higher elevations and the heads of the canyons. The hogs didn't seem to mind the worms inside the acorns. Limestone reefs contained some small fossils which were intriguing to me and it's said limestone provides minerals for good antler growth of the deer that inhabit the region.

Glen took us to the hunting area in his recently acquired used Chevy pick-up. A younger brother of one of the guys, Richard, joined us, so there were five people in our group. The three older guys occupied the front seat, while Richard and I enjoyed the open-air ride in the back of the truck. Riding in a pick-up bed was common practice back then. Police never bothered anybody about that. As we bounced along, I realized that Richard was a slow thinker, but he was a nice kid and easy to like.

Somehow, as is usual for such a large group, we were delayed in departing Tucson, so most of our drive into the mountains was after sunset.

The Whetstones run more or less north and south with a main creek cutting through just south of the center of the range. We would be camping on the main drainage and walking up ridges east and west of there, looking for wild hogs.

We located the ramshackle old line shack that Glen had permission to use for the weekend. A creek with good, drinkable water ran nearby. No big mining operations had contaminated that pristine, but desolate, area.

Upon entering the old cabin, our flashlights revealed a littered mess. Amidst old chewed-up cardboard boxes and paper, we saw lots of rat poop, grass, and other indications that rodents had long since laid claim to the premises. The three older guys cleaned it up some and got a fire going in the rock fireplace, while Richard and I gathered firewood, but the weather was clear, so I resolved to sleep in the back of the truck, clear of rodent sewage.

The area we hunted the first day.

The season opened Saturday morning, so we got up early, slapped together some quick baloney and mustard sandwiches, and struck off with our lunches and water canteens in different directions. Richard hunted with me.

We walked to the west, climbed up over a saddle, turned south, and hunted all day, mostly walking with short rest periods during which I glassed for javelina, but sighted exactly none. We did find plenty of pig sign, especially in the large patches of prickly pear cactus. The large flat "leaves" or "ears" of the prickly pear had a moth-eaten appearance from being fed on by the wild hogs. We encountered some cottontail rabbits that day and at dusk I watched a Bobcat poking around for his supper. But the cat was too far away to stalk or try to shoot. My pockets were stuffed full of interesting rocks, some of which showed small fossils.

Hot dogs and canned beans were planned for the evening meal. As Richard and I came down off the saddle we saw smoke rising from the shack's chimney. The older guys were already roasting their wienies and had cans of beans lying in the coals.

Collared Peccarys like to eat prickly pear cactus pads.

Beans and other canned food heat best by putting the unopened cans directly in the fire, but one must be alert for the "bleep" sound that occurs shortly before the can is ready to explode. Upon hearing the bleep, the can must be removed from the heat and allowed to cool for a few minutes before it is opened. Heated in this manner, the contents are uniformly warmed without burning. If the container is opened before or during heating, the contents will spill over the top and the stuff in the the bottom will be burned. If the can is not removed from the heat soon after the bleep, it will explode, making a mess, ruining the food and often causing burns or food shrapnel wounds to anyone nearby. I learned this from a smoke jumper. I never saw a can explode, but I heard stories of such neglectful occurrences.

Realizing that we had no roasting sticks, I sent Richard out to cut some for us while the others told their stories. Glen and Harold had each scored on an adult javelina, the carcasses of which were hanging from a scrub oak near the cabin. Larry had missed several shots but was enthusiastic about going back in the morning.

Harold was from back east somewhere and was really excited about this hunt and the wild, remote place we were hunting.

After filling up on hot dogs and beans, Harold had to try some fresh javelina meat, roasted on a stick over the hearth fire. He seasoned the meat with salt, pepper, and cayenne. Each of us got a piece to roast. We all agreed that the wieners tasted better. My Mom could make javelina taste great in a stew or stir fry, but this stick roasting left a lot to be desired and a very tough chew.

Not to be deterred by the first attempt, Harold sliced up the heart and divided it between us. It was better than the other meat, to my taste. It was like a chicken gizzard in texture, if not flavor.

The day had been warm and I had worked up a sweat. After supper, I felt a chill. The little shack with the fireplace in use was inviting, so I moved in with the rest of the gang. The older guys were still talking and laughing as I drifted off to sleep.

We were all up before daylight and soon off on the hunt. Richard and I went up to the same saddle, then turned north to see a different area. There was an increasing abundance of hog signs the further north we walked. I told Richard we had to be quiet and very careful as this was our last chance to get a pig. We went down the slope of a large draw and were nearly at the crest of the opposite side when I saw some pigs not very far up ahead of us. I levered a shell into the chamber and told Richard to do the same. He had the same Model 94 carbine as I was carrying, but his was a 30/30. I told him to not pull back the hammer until he was ready to shoot. Then we tiptoed toward the hogs, being especially careful to not dislodge any of the scattered rocks. As we approached them from downhill I could see one or two animals only occasionally as they rummaged around in their breakfast feeding on the cactus patch. We continued our slow creep up the slope. There was no wind. The pigs were not aware of our presence.

Suddenly just about twenty yards in front of us, several pigs exploded out of a big prickly pear patch, grunting and running in all directions. One pig came running toward me, so I cocked the hammer and fired. The pig dropped to the ground. Richard shot two times but hollered that he had missed. I don't know how he could have seen the pigs from his position which was well behind me and lower on the slope.

"Get one fer me, get one fer me, too," he yelled.

Richard was to the right of me and below. I saw the back of another pig running crossways from my right to left near the pig I had knocked down. I held for the front part of the pig and squeezed. The javelina dropped.

Waiting to see what would happen next, I stood where I was. Richard was coming to me. Another pig - the biggest one I had seen that day - came running up from below us and jumped right over Richard's dead hog and kept going. After seeing the big one, I wished I had not shot either of the small ones previously. Then everything was quiet.

We each had a javelina lying dead on the ground.

We grabbed them by their hind legs and drug them out of the cactus patch to an open grassy spot. They were not adult pigs, but, oh well, we got 'em.

Using my wonderful K-bar sheath knife, I gutted both of the young hogs, but left the hearts, lungs, and liver attached and inside the chest cavities. I tied the front and hind legs together to make a sling and we each carried our kills back to the cabin. Hanging next to the pigs taken the day before, our animals were embarrassingly small. Gutted, mine weighed fourteen pounds and Richard's tipped the scales at eight. An adult Javalina boar can go up to fifty pounds field dressed.

I noticed that my pig only had one dew claw on each hind foot. It was on the inside of the back of the foot. Figuring I had a freak, I checked the other animals and found the same situation. I've always wondered why evolutionary advantage favored the loss of the outboard dew claw on the hind feet.

My Timex wristwatch showed just past one o'clock. We returned to the shack early and ate our sandwiches in the shade of the tree holding our game. After two hours we heard our partners coming up the canyon. They had a pig. When they saw us, at first they did not realize that we had both scored. Upon seeing our pigs they all let out some wild whoops and congratulated us. They said they were feeling bad that we had not all hunted together as they encountered a huge herd of pigs and wished we had been there to get ours, but everything turned out well for our party. No one mentioned the diminutive size of our trophy hogs.

An adult Javalina, or Collared Peccary.

Without much delay, we loaded up the truck and started back to town. We were treated to some good daylight views on our way out of the mountains which had been denied us on the way in.

When we got to a gas station at Vail, Glen called my Dad. We planned to meet at Oracle Road. We stopped at the first McDonald's and Harold bought hamburgers and milkshakes for the whole gang.

What a great hunt it had been for everyone!

After telling Dad about the events of the weekend I fell asleep shortly after leaving Tucson.

## THE NEXT YEAR

My little sister, Pat, was five years younger but she showed real interest in hunting and fishing, so everyone encouraged her. When Pat was in fifth grade Dad had a weekend free during Javalina season, so we three planned to go pig hunting. I loaned her my .32 Special and I used Pop's bolt action 8mm Mauser. We each shot a few times with the unfamiliar weapons and Dad decided we shot them well enough. If we were able to get two pigs, that would be plenty as Mom would cook them, but she preferred deer, rabbits, and most other wild game to Javalina.

We left town about an hour before sunup and drove to the San Pedro River, then up one of the difficult, sandy, ranch roads toward the Galiuro Mountains. We drove along the road that followed a ridge line and watched the canyons on either side, stopping frequently to glass for pigs. Dad was hoping to find some within sight of the road, so as not to spoil the whole hunting effort for Pat by working too hard and walking a long distance. But we sighted no hogs, so when we ran into a lot of freshly chewed prickly pear cactus, some of which were still dripping juice, Dad decided we should park the truck and go on foot in search of the critters that recently chewed the cactus. Pat was tough and determined to keep up without complaining.

We walked down into the big wash to the north of the road, seeing fresh tracks and recently munched prickly pear cactus all along the way. It wasn't much past sunrise. Across the dry sand wash and halfway up the opposite side we counted fourteen pigs feeding and occasionally growling at each other.

During deer season we had encountered javelina before they got out of their overnight pile. The pigs have only long bristly hairs which provide minimal warmth, so at night they pile up together to benefit from each other's body heat. This drove of hogs had only recently left their bed.

We stalked carefully with the wind in our faces until we were within forty yards of the myopic, browsing omnivores. Dad nodded at Pat to shoot when she was ready. She stood offhand and fired. Her target just stood there, shaking its head. I shot at one of the larger hogs as it ran angling away from me, hitting it in the withers and anchoring it. Pat's target was acting woozy, but still on its feet, so she shot again, dropping it this time.

Pat's first shot had hit the javelina in the mouth, ruining the impressive set of canine teeth it had. My pig was a bit larger and had its jaws still intact. I planned to boil the head, eat the head meat, and clean the skull up for display on my bedroom wall. And that's what I did. This was Pat's first big game animal.

Me and Pat with our Javelina

## THE BOMB SHELTER

My Dad was a Mining Engineer, and he loved to work underground. That subterranean bit did not rub off on me. The thought of being buried deep in the bowels of the earth were not welcome. Also, immediately following an underground blast, I got an instant, severe headache.

But I got to thinking about the possibility of a nuclear bomb attack on the USA by the Ruskies and I thought that going underground might be the best - or only - bet for survival in such a circumstance. There was talk of the government putting in some missile silos about 30 miles west of our town.

So I asked Pop about the feasibility of building a family bomb shelter. We were renting a house from the mining company and did not own the land, but that did not dissuade my Dad from helping me plan a family survival shelter, or bunker.

Pop was never one to just brush off ideas proposed by me, even if they sounded out of reach or were just plain crazy kid ideas.

"Maybe we ought to look into this. Let's get some plans put on graph paper and do some cost estimates," Pop suggested. Of course, this would involve me and force me to investigate and evaluate the whole scenario. My Dad was great at such indirect methods of getting me involved in depth in things with which I would not normally want to deal.

My Dad was skilled at drafting on graph paper and the project proved to be an interesting and enlightening one, especially for me. Later in life, I would design every building I constructed on graph paper. We had no television or other such modern distractions back then, in the 1950s. I had books, games, bikes, and a single-shot .22 rifle, but those activities left me with spare time.

Soon I was ready to go with the project and envisioned a snug, comfortable shelter of reinforced concrete and concrete blocks, dug into the hard caleche with a discretely hidden air vent, a pantry full of food, and a well-stocked gun and ammunition rack.

I reckoned we'd need a radio and a good supply of books, maybe a good pan for making popcorn and supplies for cookies and pies. Maybe we could someday get a television set and rig that up, even though we didn't even own one yet for the house.

'Course we'd accommodate the dog and cat, maybe have room and provisions for selected neighbors and friends, - as long as they were females, I figured. I kept the last qualifying caveat to myself.

The project consumed my evenings for a couple of weeks. I spent hours at the school library (the little company town had no public library), I discussed the plans with my math and science teachers. I studied concrete foundations and how to pour solid walls and roofs with reinforcing iron bars. If no re-bar was available, wire or linear scraps of metal would do. I looked into water procurement which was a real issue in the desert area where we lived. I studied methods of keeping meat and vegetables from spoiling without the use of electricity. We'd need plenty of salt. Jerky or pemmican would have to be a dietary staple for us. We would have to learn to live without ice cream!

It was going to take a considerable amount of sheltered space to store enough food to keep the family going for several weeks. We'd need to depend on propane to cook and Blazo to fuel our Coleman lanterns. Fuel supply could be simplified by just using Blazo. It was not going to be very easy ... or pleasant. I hoped that the nuclear fall-out would not be so severe that we had to spend more than a couple of weeks or maybe a month or so in the shelter, before we could head into the mountains.

This business of taking on the responsibilities of a modern-day Noah was proving to be anything but fun.

After a couple of months of drafting the layout and estimating the costs of materials, the minimum outlay would be more than $7,000 for even a small-sized bunker. Shoot! That was going to make the project prohibitively expensive!

In the mid-1950s, a new Ford car could be had for a couple of thousand dollars or less. I recall Pop telling me that a new Cadillac might cost over $5,000!

If we should decide to move again, the bomb shelter would have to be left behind to probably be seized by the mining company for its big shots, anyway. In fact, I worried, that when the company officials saw what a secure bunker we had built, they might confiscate it for their own use, force us to move away, and all our work and expense would have been for naught. So it is when one does not own the land he lives on.

We decided that with the missile silos being constructed not too far from our little town and the SAC bombers on constant alert, maybe we should leave this bomb shelter business to the government, after all.

But the thought of a nuclear holocaust kept entering my consciousness ... and my dreams.

I often sat bored in class looking across the valley at the distant Galiuro mountains and daydreaming of how, if the big blast came, I would gather up as many pretty girls, maybe twenty head - a dozen or two at least - some of whom should be good cooks or seamstresses - as I could, along with my dog, Gyp, my single shot .22, a shotgun and a larger caliber rifle and plenty of ammunition before heading for the hills. There would be a lot of gear to pack a long distance, so I'd better have at least a couple dozen girls to help with that, along with their other duties. The Galiuro Mountains to the east looked like the best place to me, as I knew of a few caves and several old mine shafts that could serve as temporary shelters. Plus the old mining areas often had discarded steel and other materials that would be immensely helpful in our reconstruction of a civilized society, and my huge new family!

Then, after I had a deer or two hung up, I'd seriously go about my duties of repopulating the earth. I considered the possibility that I might even begin that demographic renewal project even before I had any meat hung up. Why, I might begin before we even left town!

But the bomb was never dropped and I never got the chance! Such are the dreams of schoolboys.

In 2007, at my 47-year High School reunion, I told this story and got a few chuckles. Later, during a ladies' choice dance with a formerly homely schoolmate who had matured into an especially attractive woman, she asked me if I would have waited with the repopulating efforts in her case. I told her no, as she would definitely have caused me to neglect the meat harvest, - at least for a while.

## Back for more Bass

It had taken way too much time for Dick and me to get back to our secret fishing hole. A couple of months had passed. It seemed that one or the other of us, for some reason or another, could not go, but we honored our pledge to keep the secret between just the two of us. Finally, synchrony of our schedules became possible. We packed big lunches, filled our canteens, mounted our bicycles, and headed down to the river, full of hope and anticipation of catching some dandy bass. This time Dick had a Heddon River Runt plug of his own. We each carried an old cloth flour sack to conceal our catch.

Plumes of dust rose behind us as we sped down the dirt road on our bicycles toward the pond. A mile out of town, we saw a large mule deer buck, but ignored it. We were betting on who would catch the first fish and who would pull in the monster that we saw jump and get the dragonfly.

We carefully hid our bikes on the town side of the river, just off the road, and then charged off at a run to our wonderful pond.

This time things were different. Before we crossed the fence we saw a light in the old house that sat in a grove of cottonwood and large mesquite trees that were about a football field distant from the pond. Someone was there.

Deciding we should look the situation over before we crossed the fence, we stashed our fishing poles and gear and maneuvered outside the fence to get closer to the house. We watched for what seemed like a long time, but it was probably not more than a few minutes. With finny temptations so close, the time seemed to drag for us. Tasty Bass were calling us. After seeing no one, we retrieved our gear and headed for the pond.

Dick and I each got a nice bass on our first cast. It seemed those fish were bored and waiting for us to come to entertain them. We had to work for our next ones, but after a few minutes, we had two apiece. They were all the same size - about two and a half to three pounds. Then we saw a man coming our way. He had seen us and was hollering at us to get away from his pond. We grabbed our fish and ran for the fence. I dropped one of mine and turned back to retrieve it. The man was running and cussing a blue streak, but we were through the barbed wire and soon into the brush and out of sight. We could still hear him swearing at us. He wasn't happy.

Fearing the grouchy old man might get in a vehicle and drive to the road near where we had hidden our bikes, we hung out in the dense thicket for some time. Then, becoming antsy for something to do, we went to Indian Hill, next to the borrow pit, to search for arrowheads. We could keep an eye on the road and the river bed from that prominence. The Indians had chosen their village site well. There was seldom much traffic down along the river, but that afternoon three or four cars came through. All of them came from the town side, so we figured they were not looking for us.

We kept taking our beautiful fish out to admire them. After a couple of hours, the fish began to dry out, so we gutted them, pulled some grass, wet it down plenty, and packed it around the fish. They kept very well that way.

We ate our lunches and, with pockets full of broken Indian pottery and flint flakes, we got on our bikes and headed home.

This time we accepted a ride up the hill to town. The fellow asked why we had fishing poles as there was nothing but tiny Gila minnows in the San Pedro. We told him that we just wanted to try. It was good he couldn't see the bass in our sacks.

Once again, I had enough fish to feed the whole family. Dad asked where I was getting those beauties, but I told him I had to keep the secret between Dick and myself. Dad just nodded his head.

Less than a month later we were back at the pond. We scrutinized the area and seeing no sign of people, we got right to business with the fishing. Like the time before, we each immediately hooked a nice bass. We were heads down and bent over our catches when we heard the old man yell again. He hoarsely yelled that he was going to turn his dog loose on us blankety-blank trespassers. Dick and I gathered up our gear and sprinted for the fence.

Dropping on my back to better watch for the dog and avoid the barbs, I slid underneath and was on my way to the thicket when I heard Dick holler that he was caught in the wire. I dropped my pole and pack and ran back to help him. He had tried to crawl under. Sure enough, the back of his shirt was snagged on two barbs. The dog was barking and coming full tilt at us. As I jerked his shirt free of the wires, the dog grabbed his pant leg and began to shake its head violently. This dog appeared to be trained. Dick was kicking with his other foot and screeching while I pulled on his arms. I could hear the old man yelling and cussing as he came our way. After prolonged seconds of struggle, Dick was free and we both ran like scared rabbits for the heavy brush, carrying our fishing poles and illicit catch along. I thought I heard a shotgun blast and was worried that big dog would catch us. I had a flashing thought of the story of the Hound of the Baskervilles, by Arthur Conan Doyle.

We were probably the most rattled pair of thirteen-year-olds in North America - maybe the whole world - at the moment.

We didn't quit running until we got atop Indian Hill. Again I reflected on the old Indians having their village there, giving a clear view of anyone approaching from the surrounding country, as we kept a careful watch, expecting trouble from the profane old geezer and his attack dog. After guzzling our water we devoured a sandwich and checked to be sure we had our fish, - we still had 'em, so we gutted them and packed them in wet grass.

Before we left the hill I noticed that in addition to the two holes, Dick had blood on the back of his shirt. He pulled it up and revealed an inch-long gash in his skin. He hadn't noticed it before I mentioned it, but it became very painful after I brought it to his attention. He noticed that he had leaked a considerable amount of blood and the sight of his own blood scared him, I guess.

This escapade had to be kept secret, too. We assumed that the ornery old man owned the pond and house, but we agreed that we needed to try to find out all we could about that aggressive madman.

It may have been some form of cosmic justice that we got no ride up the three-mile-long hill to town that day.

At school the next day, Dick was bent over, favoring the deep scratch on his back. He acted like a severely wounded soldier. Being as discreet as we could without divulging our trespass, or our secret fishing hole we searched for information about the pond and the crazy old person who lived there. One kid from a ranch down the valley told us that the rancher who owned or leased that part of the river bottom had hired a retired old geezer to stay in the house. So Dick and I surmised that maybe the old boy just liked fish and wanted to keep them all for himself. We debated how we might tap that treasure house of fishing fun at less risk of bodily damage.

Before we had drummed up enough courage to go back to the pond, we heard a rumor that the caretaker of an area down on the river was a recently released convict who had been pardoned from a life sentence for torturing and murdering children. That had to be our man! Somehow, the issue of returning to our fishing pole just never came up again.

I wondered if the old boy didn't spread the rumor to rid himself of our fish-raiding sorties.

## MEAN COW

I used the school library to learn the difference between hares and rabbits. They are both leporids. Hares are substantially larger than rabbits, have longer ears, and are less social than bunnies. A hare's pregnancy lasts 42 days, compared with rabbits' 30-31 days with a bunny litter in the oven. Newborn hares, called leverets, are fully developed at birth—furred with open eyes—while newborn rabbits, called kittens or kits, are born undeveloped, with closed eyes, no fur, and an inability to regulate their own temperature. Their nests are also worlds apart—"hares live completely aboveground, lacking the normal burrow or warren system of rabbits." Probably most significantly, hares are able to see, eat, and run at birth and do not use burrows.

The cactus-blighted desert surrounding the big new copper mine in southern Arizona where my Dad worked had an abundance of cottontail rabbits, along with some jack rabbits - which are actually hares. So beginning shortly after we arrived, I often took a short stroll in the nearby desert after school to go hunting with my Dad's single-shot .22 rifle. Most weeks I would get out once or twice, depending on how many rabbits I'd taken, and how many Mom or the neighbors could use. I was twelve years of age when I began this "market hunting" enterprise. A box of fifty .22 short bullets cost about fifty cents and a single .22 short round could produce a rabbit worth a dollar, or sometimes two bucks for head-shot ones, from the neighbors, so it was good business for me, even if I missed head shots now and then. I never tired of hunting and so far, more than seventy years later, I've still never tired of hunting activities.

After several weeks of harvesting the bunnies within a few minutes of walking time from our house, I was beginning to see fewer rabbits, so I decided to use my bicycle to access more distant hunting grounds, at least until our local stock regenerated - which they normally do at a rapid rate. On some occasions, I would invite a friend to come along, but most of my buddies were good only for one or two trips before they decided they preferred other activities. Most of my friends' Moms didn't care to prepare wild rabbits for their families to eat, anyway. Chicken was available and inexpensive, ready to put in the pan. And if we weren't going to use the animal, I couldn't justify killing it. As for me, I preferred wild rabbits to domestic chickens. Many folks were scared of tularemia, but we'd never heard of anybody getting it, so we didn't worry. And no one that I knew ever used rubber gloves when butchering the rabbits.

On one trip I had pedaled alone and uphill a couple of miles up the dirt road toward the Catalina Mountains to an area that I hadn't hit before. I concealed my bike in some brush near the road, then climbed over the four-strand barbed wire fence and began seeing rabbits before I was out of sight of the dirt road. There were so many of the robust little critters that I decided to walk on over the nearest hill to see what might lie beyond before shooting anything. I figured I could shoot plenty on the way back and I would have to carry the dead rabbits for a shorter distance.

I noticed plenty of cow "pies" freshly plopped in that area. It appeared that one of the local ranchers had recently moved some cattle in from somewhere. That didn't matter at all to me. Range cattle were sometimes spooky, and most would charge off and away if they spotted a person on foot. I'd never experienced anything to make me fearful of beef cattle.

Until that day.

When I topped the hill I saw a dozen or more cows, most of which had a very small calf with them. They were scattered through the brush and palo verde trees, grazing on whatever tufts of windblown, desiccated grass they could find. When I got to the bottom of a little canyon I saw a mature Jack Rabbit (*Lepus alleni*) which, as previously noted, is actually a hare, rather than a rabbit. The "jacks" are much larger than the cottontails and I figured if I could get a couple of those, I'd have plenty to take home, as they weigh three or four times the two-pound weight of an average desert cottontail and they brought three dollars each from those who would eat them.

My quarry was watching the cattle when I eased along to within about thirty-five yards, drew a bead on the head, and made my shot.

The hare flopped over and began kicking wildly in its reflex-driven death throes.

An alerted Jack Rabbit

The nearest cow let out a bellow and ran directly for the thrashing hare. When she got to within a few feet of the still-twitching animal she bellowed again and began to throw her head from left to right, slinging snot in all directions. That really made her horns look dangerous, small as they were. She was slinging gobs of snot ten, maybe twenty, feet away. It seemed to me that she was looking for whatever had molested that hare. The angry old cow began to paw the sand, with her bewildered calf close behind.

I remained frozen, hunched down next to a thickly branched palo verde tree. I was happy for the concealment it provided and relieved that I was downwind of the enraged bovine.

The cow seemed to gather her resolve before she cautiously approached the by-then, lifeless carcass of the hare. Gingerly the bovine nearly touched the hare with its nose, then gave a loud snort, wheeled, and charged off a few yards before stopping to look back at the bloody hare. It seemed the cow did not like the smell of blood. To me, the old heifer seemed to have a fire, or maybe it was blood in her eyes.

One very angry cow.

Common sense told me to remain absolutely still and obscured amidst the branches of the tree until the infuriated cow departed. The upset old heifer turned and walked away a few steps, then wheeled around to stare again at the hare carcass as she shook her head. Then she turned and walked a few more steps, before abruptly turning around to look again at the lifeless bunny. She was not easily satisfied.

I had never before seen such behavior from any bovine. I had no idea what she might do next, so I remained frozen in place.

The old cow weighed about four or five hundred pounds and she could make my life miserable if she located me and decided to do so. I wanted no close-up battle with her and those horns.

But time was ticking by and I had a long ride home and had expected to collect more than one hare for my effort.

The calf had been lagging behind its mother and when the cow let forth a raspy bellow the calf scrambled up the hillside and continued on over the skyline and out of sight. The cow trotted on to catch up to her offspring.

That was my cue to make a dash over to retrieve the hare and head back the way I came. But as I picked up the jackrabbit that ornery cow came back to the top of the hill, saw me, and let out a bellow as she came running down clunking through the loose rocks of the hillside. This time her attention was definitely focused on me. That cousin to a wild ox seemed bent on my destruction. Only about one hundred yards separated me from what I knew could be a horrible stomping - maybe a goring, too. Her horns seemed to become more prominent the closer she came to me.

The ruckus and racket had alerted the other cattle and two more curious cows with newborn calves trotted toward me.

Another alert, horned, and curious cow.

The palo verde tree that had concealed me was not large enough for me to climb to escape the hooves and horns of my dedicated pursuer, nor was there any other potential refuge in sight.

Additionally, it was springtime and the palo verdes had fresh green spikes, many of which would impale me most painfully if I attempted to climb one. I would have to run as fast as I could in hopes of locating a safe place, but I realized my only real safety would be on the other side of the barbed wire fence.

With my Dad's single shot .22 in one hand and the dead hare in the other, I ran up the hill with the aggressive cow and how many others I was not sure, in hot pursuit. I could hear them coming and knew I could not stay ahead of them for long.

I topped out on the little hill and with about two hundred yards separating me from the fence, I knew I couldn't get there before being overtaken by that cow. I flashed on a mental image of me and the body of the hare being stomped into a soupy mess of meat, bone, hare's ears, blood, and my plaid shirt. Fleeting though it was, the thought left an indelible impression on me.

To the right of my most direct route of flight was a clump of five or six yucca plants. They were only about three feet high, but they just might conceal me. If the cow found me there, I would be in a bad way, but surely no worse off than if she overtook me on my direct route to the fence. So I made an abrupt hook to the right and hunkered down amidst the yucca spines and a huge pack rat nest. It was late afternoon and I was mindful of the potential of a snake being in or near the nest, but my quick glance revealed no danger.

Lucky for me, the wind was coming from the cow to me, so her nose would not aid her in locating my whereabouts.

The panting cow loomed up over the crest of the hill with her tongue hanging out and continued on a straight tack down the slope, without even a glance at my temporary resting place. I debated shooting her in the forehead if she returned, but the thought of having to pay for a cow and maybe a calf too dissuaded me from seriously considering such extreme defensive action. I figured if I shot the calf, that might enrage the cow even more, so that idea was no good either. Plus I could probably heal up from a stomping sooner than I could save up enough money to cover the cost of even just a calf.

My position on my hands and knees in the rocks, contorted to avoid the spines of the yucca leaves, was cramped and my view of the immediate surroundings was compromised, so after a minute or so, I eased up to get a better look through the yucca growth. A striped whiptail lizard stuck its head out of the rat's nest, saw me, blinked an eye, and then quickly withdrew.

The cow had stopped her headlong charge and was moving slowly among some palo verde trees and patches of prickly pear cactus downhill from me. She seemed to be searching for something - I was sure that would be me. I was closer to the barbed wire fence than I was to the cow, but I decided to sit tight in the hope of improvement in my situation.

The lizard quickly disappeared.

To add to my predicament, a slight thermal breeze was by then taking my scent straight toward the angry bovine.

The calf eventually caught up to its mother and began to jab its nose into the udder of the cow, wanting to nurse. I wasn't concerned about the other cattle, none of which were in sight, assuming that their behavior would be normal, but that ornery cow was still plenty twitchy. Finally, the calf's incessant poking caused the mother to settle down and stand still while the calf sucked. With the cow's back turned to me I eased up and began a cautious, bent-over creep toward the fence line.

When I was about halfway to the fence the cow looked back and saw me, kicked at her calf, which bawled. The cow came toward me on a run. I'd never before run into such a nightmarishly mean cow.

I went into high gear too, but I could see that I was not going to make the fence in time to get over it before the cow overtook me. I sure didn't like the thought of being gored as I was going over the top wire. I stopped about ten yards short of the wire and as the cow came in, shaking her head and throwing snot to both sides, I flung the hare carcass at her.

That stopped her. I made a running dive to propel myself under the bottom wire of the fence and nearly made it, but two barbs pierced my Levi jacket and I was stopped halfway under the wire with the cow back on her trajectory, aiming to do me evil.

I could hear her hooves clattering through loose rocks as she came at me. As I scrambled, I somehow bumped my forehead on the forepiece of my rifle and tore loose from the wire just as the cow reached the fence. She struck at me with a front foot. It missed me, but her leg got hung between the bottom and the second strand of wire. She bellowed and attacked the fence with her horns until the rusty bottom wire broke and set her free.

By then I was hunkered down in the brush where I'd hidden my bicycle, wondering what would come next. I dreaded her coming through that fence.

The calf came to its mother and began nosing again. The cow had enough of the barbed wire and walked back the way she had come with her calf trailing close behind.

Well, I was rattled, missing one jackrabbit and facing a long ride home which would end in the dark, but the road was mostly downhill from there. As I peddled along I wondered what the remains of that jackrabbit looked like.

When I walked into the kitchen, my Mom asked how I got the lump on my head. I told her, "Mean cow, Mom."

## GILA MONSTERS

My first encounter with a Gila Monster took place as we drove from Trench Mine to Tucson to shop and visit the traveling Circus. It was about 1952. We were traveling north through some dry desert area when we saw the huge lizard on the road. Dad slowed the car immediately and we came to a stop next to the colorful critter which continued its ponderous pace toward the side of the pavement.

"Let's catch it," I hollered, but Mom shouted that no one would touch the thing. So we watched the dreadful-looking beast as it methodically marched on and disappeared into a bush.

This lizard wasn't giving ground to anybody.

But I was certain I could single-handedly catch a monster like that and I looked forward to my first opportunity to do so.

I believe Gila Monsters are not commonly seen anyplace, except in zoos. Eight years passed before I encountered one again. As I was coming home from hunting Mourning Doves near Oracle, Arizona I noticed an abundance of Doves near a large cattle water trough. It was a hot day. Hunting had been slow and there was about a half hour of light left, so I parked the truck and took my shotgun to the trough. Close to the water container I saw the monster. It was intent on trying to swallow a small rodent. I walked right up to the fat lizard and used the butt of my shotgun to pin the head down, then I picked it up. I was impressed with how powerful the beast was! With monster writhing in my right hand I headed for the truck, emptied my bag of birds into the bed of the pickup and put the lizard in the bag, then tied off the bag with a piece of twine.

The fierce-looking beast was muscular and powerful as it squirmed in my grip. Once in the bag it began to hiss. Its breath was worse than that of the ugliest girl in my class. It was two pounds of ugly, stinking, muscular, malevolence.

At home, after skinning the doves, I emptied the monster out of the bag. Apparently, it had completely swallowed the rodent and as soon as its feet felt the grass, it began hissing angrily. I was surprised at how much noise emanated from that nasty-natured lizard. My Mom was not pleased to have the beast near our home and pointedly told me to take it into the desert away from town and release it. I had only begun to investigate the thing, and I wanted to observe it for a few days, then maybe skin it, but Mom was serious, so I complied.

After the passing of my wife, Mae in 1983, I was headquartered near my Uncle Stan's home and corrals west of Tucson during part of the winter.. His son, Steve, was anxious to engage in outdoor activities, especially those involving animals. One afternoon as Steve came home from the school bus stop he told me there was a Gila Monster in the yard near the corrals. I went with him, easily caught the lizard, and then handed it to Steve.

This was one tough lizard.

In late August 1960, I drove to Tucson to see the Cardiac specialist about my heart murmur I encountered a large Gila Monster crossing the pavement near Oracle Junction. It looked like the largest one I had ever seen. I easily caught the two-foot-long beast and put it in the bed of the pickup. Soon I noticed that it was standing near one corner of the tailgate with its nose just at the rim. I tapped the brakes and the lizard fell back into the bed. This scenario was repeated several times on the forty-minute drive to the animal buyer. I dropped it off at the wild animal buyer's place in Tucson and was told that it was forbidden to molest Gila Monsters in any manner, including catching, but he would release it for me, so I thanked them and left it for him to deal with.

It was a small one.

## Boy Scouts, Seventh Grade

While still living in Socorro, New Mexico, I had been a Cub Scout and enjoyed most of the activities. Of course I started as a Bobcat, then went to Wolf, Bear, and Lion rank, but I had not been around any clubs since we moved.

When we first got to San Manuel I was invited to visit a meeting of one of the Boy Scout troops. The scout master's house was only a few blocks from our house, so despite my natural reluctance to do group things, I walked over to see what it was all about. I was immediately sold on the whole program. I joined that first meeting.

Eldon Porter, the Scout Master, was a truly admirable man. He exuded self-confidence and inspired it in all his troops. We sang songs, practiced the Boy Scout motto - "Be Prepared," and had really enjoyable, useful, instructive meetings. Best of all, camping trips were discussed and planned to take place on weekends and vacation breaks. I began working on accumulating Merit Badges, which were the means by which I could become more competent in the outdoors, and ascend into the higher ranks of the organization. It was appropriate merit-based advancement, as I believe all advancement should be.

So, I began as a Tenderfoot, soon was a Second Class, then a First Class Boy Scout. Each successive rank required more experience and merit badges along with service to the troop and other people, camping trips, and good conduct. We were all expected to be Brave, Clean, and Reverent - at all times.

Reciting the Pledge of Allegiance was always a pleasure to me, as was the Boy Scout Oath.

> *On my honor, I will do my best*
> *To do my duty to God and my country, and to obey the Scout Law;*
> *(what all that included none of us knew for sure)*
> *To help other people at all times;*
> *To keep myself physically strong, mentally awake and morally straight.*

Duty to God, Country, other people, and, lastly, myself, all appealed to me.

To me, the scout oath was similar in importance to the Apostles' Creed which we recited in church.

But most other ceremonies and rituals I was never very enthusiastic about.

At the meetings, I especially enjoyed learning and using the various knots and other practical things.

After only a few months I had earned the six merit badges required to become a Star Scout. From there I progressed through the rank of Life and finally, I became the first kid in San Manual to become an Eagle Scout when I was a Sophomore in High School. That was just a couple of months before I was kicked out of school for fighting too much. I was proud of my uniform and sash and pleased to present Mom with new merit badges, which she was happy to stitch onto the sash.

The camping trips were the best part of scouting as far as I was concerned and the best of those were the ones to Arivaipa Canyon. We older scouts were expected to look out for the younger boys, but some teasing was tolerated - it was even expected.

Mr. Porter was also a leader of the local Mormon Church, in fact, he was a Bishop. The Church of Jesus Christ of Latter Day Saints (LDS) had lots of wholesome activities for kids - and also some very pretty girls. I began to attend some of their dances and other activities. My parents thought that was fine, as there was never any booze at any of their shindigs.

## Camping at Aravaipa Canyon

Aravaipa (or Arivaipa - I thought it should mean "every viper") Creek and Canyon were in the Galiuro Mountains a few miles north and east of the town of Mammoth, which was located down on the San Pedro River, which ran, when it ran, a bit to the northeast of San Manuel (I never found the "salmon well"). In the 1950s Aravaipa was a popular spot to visit and far enough away from town to make camping desirable. The creek ran clear and had more water than the San Pedro River, except for brief periods in August when heavy rains filled the larger river.

A narrow gorge nearly conceals the wonderful Aravaipa Creek as it runs out of a spectacular deep canyon with sheer rock walls on both sides. It is a true oasis in the dry, rocky, cactus-filled desert scrubland. The cottonwood, willow, walnut, juniper, sycamore, palo verde trees, and good grasses have drawn people to the canyon for eons. Tall saguaro cacti stand as silent entrance sentinels to that special place.

We were told that Aravaipa Creek had seven species of native fish. On our camping trips, we never failed to see fish of six to twelve inches in length that looked like trout to us, but they were called Chubs.

Big game inhabiting the canyon included Desert Bighorn Sheep, Mule deer, Mountain Lions, Javelina, and in the higher elevations, Coes White-tailed Deer. An assistant Scout Master, familiar with the place, told us that we could expect to see, or at least see signs of, Javalina, Bobcat, Coati Mundi, Cottontail rabbits, Jack Rabbit (Hares), both Red and Grey Foxes, Badgers, Skunks, and maybe even a Raccoon. We practiced with books from the library and were prepared to decipher any track that we encountered.

We were cautioned that tarantulas, scorpions, centipedes, and snakes, of course, were all part of the natural fauna and we were to be especially careful and holler to the adults if we found any of those. Bugs of that sort and all snakes naturally spook people. I had partially overcome my innate fear of snakes and bugs. At least I had it under control, but most of my young companions did not.

At a scout meeting before one of our camping trips to Aravaipa, an older cowboy from one of the local ranches came to town. Someone told him that a bunch of young scouts was planning a trip to Arivaipa and would like to hear from him about his knowledge and experience in that area in the previous century. He agreed to come to the meeting.

The old cowboy spent a long evening telling us about the area and the people of the century before - back in the 1800s. He told us about the Arivaipa Apaches, who occupied the area when white men (anglos) first saw it. He told us that about eighty years ago (the cowboy looked like he was at least eighty years old), the chief of the Arivaipas, named Eskiminzin, was the leader of the band of up to five hundred Apaches. They did some farming along the Arivaipa and used mescal, also known as agave or century plant extensively for food and concocted a fermented drink from it called *Tizwin*.

Water does wonders in desert country.

There were lots of different bands, or tribes, of Apaches. Many did not get along with other bands of their own tribe and most Apaches did not care for other Indian tribes or Mexicans. Apaches were generally a pretty mean, aggressive lot, he told us

The U.S. Army had a cavalry post, called Camp Grant, where Aravaipa Creek entered the San Pedro River. This post was just a hastily assembled, scattered collection of adobe houses. They were no more than hovels, in fact.

The fort at the junction of Aravaipa Creek and the San Pedro River, primarily a miserable collection of small adobe buildings, was to provide security for the increasing numbers of settlers and miners in this area of the Arizona territory. But continuous bitter guerrilla warfare between Apaches and the Mexicans had gone on for nearly two hundred years. Raiding was the Apache's preferred method, and it also became a way of life. Apache did not keep or breed herds of cattle. They did not keep and breed horses like the plains Indian tribes did. Cattle captured in raids were used for food, and mules and horses were used for both transportation and food. Once the captured herds were used up, the raiders went out seeking more. Indians would then indiscriminately kill Mexican and white newcomers, sometimes after first subjecting them to torture, which motivated the Apaches, and was more for retaliation and revenge than economic gain. Over the two centuries of conflict, the Apache bands had acquired a deep distrust of outsiders. Indian raiding parties began attacking US ranches, camps, prospectors, freighters, wagon trains, stages, immigrants in small groups, and settlements of all kinds.

Camp Grant in 1871. It only existed from 1860 to 1872.

Eskiminzin had moved his people close to Camp Grant for protection from Anglos, Mexicans, and other Indians, as well as to receive food and farming implements from the government. The Indians had promised to be peaceful and go back to farming and hunting wild game. But they liked their traditional form of homebrew called Tizwin, which the army soon outlawed. Prohibition of this mildly fermented drink led to problems with the government. The Indians could get jeeped up pretty high on Tizwin, but its effects were nothing like those that came from the white man's distilled liquor or moonshine.

By early March 1871, there were 300 Aravaipa and Pinal Apache camped near Camp Grant, and by the end of March there were 500. During March the flow of Aravaipa Creek declined and Lt. Whitman authorized the Apache to move five miles upstream, away from Camp Grant, to the mouth of Aravaipa Canyon.

Multiple instances of stock rustling and murder of whites and Mexicans had taken place during the winter of 1870-1871. A few Indians had been caught with some of the stolen stock and killed. Some of the troublemakers were identified as being Arivaipa Apaches.

Local citizens asked the Army commander for protection, but he did nothing, so in late April a band of one hundred forty- eight angry Tucsonans, made up of six whites, forty-eight Mexicans and ninety-four Papago Indians secretly left town and rode for two days, traveling only at night, to Camp Grant. Early the next morning, by total surprise, they attacked the Aravaipas with rifles and clubs, killing one hundred ten women and children, eight men, and dozens of dogs. Eskiminzin and one of his children were among those that escaped the massacre.

In 1872 Col. Crook ordered that a new Fort Grant be established at the base of Mount Graham, and that "old" Camp Grant be closed. In March 1873, the site of "old" Camp Grant was finally abandoned after twelve years use.

Not long after the wholesale slaughter, Eskiminzin visited an Anglo friend of his, enjoyed a friendly meal, then stood up, drew his pistol, and killed the Anglo point blank, as partial retaliation for the Camp Grant incident. He was quoted as saying that "it was much harder to kill a friend than to kill an enemy." I realized right then, that Sicilians were not the only people to have ongoing vendettas.

Eskiminzin posing.

Two years later Eskiminzin and the remainder of his band were rounded up and quartered at the San Carlos reservation, but they took off. One of his sons-in-law, known as the Apache Kid, killed another Indian at the reservation and immediately thereafter took off into the remote and mysterious Galiuro Mountains.

Then the old cowboy told us that his father, also a cowboy, had found a guy he reckoned to be the Apache kid wth one squaw near a water hole on the west side of the mountains. His father called for them to surrender, but the Kid fired his big, long-range buffalo rifle, hitting the cowboy's horse, then he ran for cover. The squaw was running behind the Kid but she was fat and quite a bit slower. The man's father shot the squaw in the leg. Then he shot the two horses the Indians had ridden in on. He had to shoot his own horse as it was badly wounded and would not recover. After a cat-and-mouse gunfight, eventually, the cowboy said he wounded the Apache Kid just before dark. The Kid crawled off and got away in the night.

The next morning the cowboy, on foot, cautiously approached the place where the Apache Kid had been holed up and found the squaw. She had bled to death.

The cowboy walked back to the ranch, told the others what had happened, and got a fresh horse. Several men joined him to look for the Kid. After searching for a couple of days one of the men saw buzzards circling. They rode over, and found the dead body of what they reckoned to be the Kid under a small ledge by a deep gully, a mile or so from where he had been shot. The weather was hot and the body was full of maggots and bloated, so they just left it for the birds. But the cowboy picked up the .50 caliber Sharps rifle. The old man said that he still had that dandy old weapon.

Eskiminzin was captured, put in chains, and shipped off first to Alabama, then Oklahoma, before being released. He died on the San Carlos reservation in 1895.

The place where the Apache Kid died was a desolate, dry wash that was only about eighteen miles east of San Manuel.

Well, the entire troop sat spellbound as the old man told his story. No one interrupted him. We were going to be camping right in the middle of where some of this bloody action took place - just one lifetime back in time. This area was soaked with history.

I was secretly hoping to find an old rifle, some arrowheads, or who knows what - maybe even Apache bones .... maybe, even a skull!

As unattractive as this dry, cactus-infested desert was, I was becoming interested in the land and its past.

At the school library I read that the Apache Kid, supposedly, did not die until much later, so maybe the Indian that the old cowboy killed was someone else, but it sure was a fascinating tale.

There are many stories about the death of the Apache Kid, including his death in Mexico in 1890, his death near Socorro, New Mexico in 1894, and a rancher having his freshly decapitated head in western New Mexico in 1907. One story claimed he was still rustling, murdering, and raping white women in the 1920s. For sure his legacy was such that one could pick and choose how he died. I preferred the version told us by the old cowboy.

## Friday, off to Arivaipa

The long-awaited big day at last arrived. We loaded four pick-ups with twenty-four eager (and maybe wannabe Eagle) scouts, equipment, and adult drivers. The weather was sunny and warm, as usual for that locale. Most of us rode in the back of the trucks with the tents and other equipment. We were riding with the wind in our hair. One of the group mentioned that he felt like a paratrooper on D-day. I told him that as we had not been issued parachutes yet, he'd better not bail out of the truck. Two boys had their ball caps blown off, never to be seen again, but I had mine tucked safely in my Trapper Nelson pack. Most of us ended up with sunburn and chapped lips from the open-air trip.

Not far north of Mammoth we left the pavement and turned up Arivaipa Canyon Road. The country was changing faster than movie actor Lon Chaney took to morph into a werewolf - an image I mentioned several times as conditioning for my companions on this overnight trip.

We drove from Sonoran Desert scrub to desert grassland, to chaparral, and then down to the canyon creek bottom and its riparian habitat. I was eyeballing intently, looking for signs of the old Army post, an Indian village, or spooked wildlife. The cottonwood trees were huge, the cliffs tall and steep and the wonder of the place was nearly overwhelming. I think we all felt like kids in nature's finest candy shop, with the clear flowing creek being the main attraction for us, - a bunch of desert whelps.

A mile or so onto the washboard dirt road one of the kids in the second truck hollered that he hurt his fingers. He had been perched near the rear window of the cab and was grasping the top front edge of the bed. The bed and the cab were suspended to allow for independent movement of about a half inch. When the truck hit a bump, the bed was thrust forward enough to slightly mash the kid's fingers.

So our caravan of campers pulled to the side of the road and first aid in the form of a Johnson's Band-Aid was applied to the wounded scout's finger. The young scout showed his bravery. We loaded up and journeyed on - into the vast, mountainous unknown.

After we had passed several places that looked suitable to our requirements for the two overnights, the lead driver finally pulled off the primitive one-lane road and stopped. We were to set up camp in the cottonwoods near the creek.

Three of the younger scouts had to poop, so latrine manufacture was the first order of business. I had a collapsable shovel, acquired at the Army Surplus store in Tucson, so I was detailed to be in charge of digging the trenches. With my job of cleaning toilets at the drug store, I had some experience in such matters. An empty coffee can held a roll of toilet paper nicely. Paper bags were hung on nearby branches for the used toilet paper. The bags were to be collected and burned before our departure. I dug three sets of two latrine trenches to accommodate the party of twenty-eight souls. By having side-by-side sets of two latrines, it would be less spooky for those whose call of nature came after dark. There were no girls, so the separation of holes was minimal. The buddy system would be practiced for night visits to the latrine. Steeped in undaunted courage by our leaders as we had been, we'd also heard plenty of unforgettable werewolf and vampire stories, so after dark, it was comforting to have a buddy close by, as one emptied his bladder or bowels.

Mr. Porter assigned several scouts the duty of setting up the tents. Our floorless pup tents were to house four scouts each. We'd already picked our tent mates. We piled rocks and sand around the edges of the tents to avoid drafts .... and keep wild things out. Each boy in our tent had brought along a small piece of old carpet or feed sack upon which to place his sleeping bag. Inside my bag, I had secreted a three-foot piece of old garden hose. I had a special plan for that hose.

Werewolf stories were told every night.

The head of a big centipede is spooky.

Circles of rocks were arranged to contain our small cooking fires. Most of us just planned to roast wienies, but I had two cans of pork and beans to "bleep" in the fire.

When the tents were all up and the fires started, skirmish parties went forth to gather more wood for the evening and to cut walking sticks for each member. We wanted to be prepared, and we were getting there in a hurry.

Two of the younger wannabe pathfinders sang out that they had found a centipede under a dead branch. We all rushed over to see the critter, but it was only about two inches long. I was disappointed as I expected a monster of at least six or eight inches which were not uncommon in the desert.

The little bug was allowed to slither off unharmed.

But a big centipede of eight inches or more in length will grab anyone's attention. Only the head end is dangerous, but the tail end looks like it could inflict pain, too. Once I caught one while fishing for crappies and divided it into several sqirming sections each of which really excited the fish.

As the excited gang began to get with roasting their tube steaks, I placed a can of beans in my fire. Several kids questioned the act and one of the adults came along, used his stick to flip my can free of the fire, and patiently admonished me. I told him what I had in mind and he summoned Mr. Porter. Again I explained my plan and was given the go-ahead. Everyone was a bit tense and I had to shush the gang several times, straining my ears for the bleep. It would be mortifying to see the can explode on the first night of our campout. But, after a prolonged delay, finally, I heard the telltale "bleep". I flipped the can away from the fire and after a few minutes, with gloves on, I opened the lid. This was a new trick, even for Mr. Porter. I received compliments on my bushcraft.

Stories were told of ghosts, werewolves, and wild Indians. I told my friends that it was time for me to go to bed. My announcement brought forth some hoots and jeers, which I silently endured since I planned to retire early, so I could privately slip my piece of hose under the sleeping pad of one of my tent mates. Leon was my mark for this little con game.

With all the noise coming from the campfires a few feet away, I was wide awake, but feigning sleep when my companions entered the tent. They sat on their bags, removed their shoes and one even brushed his teeth. Then when my victim stuck his legs into his bag, he felt the hose underneath and yelled "SNAKE". Everyone was on their feet and on full alert as they scrambled out of the pup tent. Mr. Porter and all the other adults were at our tent in mere seconds. I was the last to vacate our quarters and probably did not show sufficient alarm. I knew I would be a prime suspect.

With a stick, Mr. Porter cautiously probed, then groped the sleeping bag and found the hose.

When he emerged from the tent, hose in hand, Mr. Porter's face was red and his hair was mussed up, looking kind of wild, like an exploding bouffant. He asked who had misplaced their piece of hose. Mr. Porter was a cool guy.

I fessed up.

"That was a good one, Mr. Jacobson." Mr. Porter looked really frazzled, but he laughed when he said it. He asked if I had any more pieces of hose or other tricks, maybe a rubber spider or something, up my sleeve.

"No, sir, that's all I could think of to bring," I reported.

The scoutmaster raised his eyebrows and nodded his head. I interpreted his demeanor to indicate my stunt was within the limits of acceptable behavior.

The kid who hollered "snake" tried to convince us all that he hadn't really been scared, but none of the rest of the boys were sold on his spiel.

The old saying from Hamlet, " I fear he doth protest too much," came to mind. It was good to have such philosophical and historical knowledge from reading Classic Comic books.

The jabbering was still going on when I drifted off to sleep.

## SATURDAY

One of the adults brought a bugle and knew how to play reveille. Our morning call was just perfect. We all felt like soldiers on a bivouac and the bugled first call bolstered our sentiments and revved up our emotions. The flag was up, and we stood at attention, saluted, gave the scout oath, and pledged allegiance to begin the day. Family, God, and Country were on our minds.

Soon the smell of bacon in the pan had everyone salivating. Of course, a significant number of eggs had been broken in transport, but parts of some were recoverable from the sticky, broken shelled, mess. It looked like scrambled eggs would be the only option. One kid's Mom had cracked his eggs at home and put them in a cylindrical olive jar. He just poured them into the pan and cooked his sunny side up. Most of us at least claimed that we preferred ours scrambled. But I took note of that thoughtful means of transporting eggs. Something good was to be learned every day.

One of the guys, Eugene by name, from my tent, stumbled and dumped an entire loaf of sliced bread onto the ground. The slices were scattered individually like a dropped deck of cards. We blew, shook, and tapped most of the sand off the slices, but still noticed the gritty texture, in spite of the butter and jam. We all thanked Eugene for the nice work on the bread.

Eugene was more than two years older than most of us. He was taller, stronger, and outweighed us by about fifty pounds, but he was not fat. He was not the sharpest academician of the lot and had been held back a couple of grades - therefore his greater age, but he was gentle-natured and I counted him as a friend. I had observed him doing some interesting stuff, indicating that he had at least a semi-functional brain.

Lunches were prepared and consisted of sandwiches made of Spam, Vienna sausages, or canned corned beef. We had a choice of butter, margarine, or mayonnaise to help lubricate the sandwiches as they slid down our throats. A piece of fruit and a candy bar (Big Hunks and Tootsie Rolls were the most popular) completed our daytime rations.

Mr. Porter called for the kid with the mashed finger, removed the band-aid, and announced that it was healing well, before applying a fresh band-aid.

We formed three squads of eight scouts, each overseen by an adult and planned to set off in different directions to reconnoiter, explore, and map the area.

Groups would set off to the North, and the South, and one squad would go up the creek bed. Of course, the creek route was preferred by everyone. Mr. Porter asked how best to assign routes. Suggestions were to have a knife or hatchet throwing contest, to see who could hurl a large rock the farthest, climb a tree the highest, and build a fire the fastest ..... the list was long, but all contests involved risk of injury. In the end, we drew straws of grass. My group got the shortest straw and therefore, the North route.

The scribe, or cartographer, in each unit, was selected for his handwriting and drawing ability and each had to be careful to accurately record the lay of the land. We used a compass and noted the direction of our travel as well as walking time on each leg of the journey. The scribe's job was to sketch points of interest, and note types of trees and other items of botanical or other interest. Animal tracks, trails, signs and sightings, and other useful information were to be recorded. Our squad chose Andy to be the scribe. Andy was happy to be the chosen one. Unbeknownst to him, most of us dreaded that job and the responsibility that went along with it. I was sure that my barely decipherable handwriting would quickly eliminate me from that position, had I been chosen.

A kid named Roy was a member of the group assigned to the river exploration. He hurried back to his tent to get a small container, which he stashed in his backpack.

Our trail markers were to be made of naturally occurring sticks, rocks, or other materials and clearly denoted on the map. We were not allowed to use any surveyor's tape, nor were we allowed to chop blaze marks on trees. Our passage was to be such that nothing was degraded or depreciated. But, we could, in some places, intentionally break a small branch to indicate that we had passed.

Only we would know the significance of our markers. Only we would know the trails until we mutually agreed to share this information with the world.

Before setting off, to get everyone in the right frame of mind, we had a short discussion on how Lewis and Clark had done such a remarkable job in their exploration of the Louisiana Territory. We were resolved to do as thorough a job as had our illustrious forefathers.

Each scout carried a walking stick for self-defense, as well as for balance on the rocky trails as we forged through the wilderness.

We all considered this to be serious business. The plan was to combine our findings to produce a master map of the area, not only to document our journey but to facilitate future exploratory efforts.

My squad was accompanied by Mr. Porter. I thought maybe he wanted to keep an eye on me, after the garden hose episode.

We threaded our way up through the brush and rocks and reached a sheer rock wall. We fanned out at the face of the obstruction until one of our group hollered that he found a break in the rocks. Tracks in an animal trail convinced us that it would lead us out of the creek bottom. Some javelina tracks were discernible in the sandy soil, so we went single-file up the narrow, rocky pathway. In places, we needed to use both our hands to ascend to the next level. Most carried light canvass backpacks, from the Army Surplus store in Tucson, but I had my Trapper Nelson. I discovered that the solid wood frame was cumbersome in the narrow places, but later it proved its worth when I loaded it with interesting discoveries.

We all noticed and most commented on the noisy, sometimes downright noxious, flatulence coming from the troop, especially as we went uphill in the morning. One fat kid (he would be referred to as a nutritional overachiever nowadays) named Morris sounded like a pony or a burro on his first run of the day. Jet propulsion was mentioned as a benefit of such discharges. Kids scrambled to avoid the position directly behind Morris. I realized I wasn't the only one who had brought beans. I also surmised that beans are prone to produce similar music whether heated or not. That was another noteworthy discovery!

There was so much to be learned on a trip like this.

We topped out and came to more open terrain with some Juniper trees, Palo Verde trees and Ocotillo. Andy, our scribe was busy and I was glad he had the job, as I spent the time poking around under rocks and fallen branches. We turned East to skirt Arivaipa canyon, but soon found a steep, rocky ravine. Rather than attempt to cross that hazardous area, we turned back to the North. I found a worn, rusty mule shoe, which was smaller and more narrow than a horseshoe. I put it in my pack sack along with some eye-catching quartz rocks.

It was time for lunch. We had each carried two canteens of water and that was a good thing, as the day was sunny and plenty warm. Most of the kids wore waist-length Levi jackets but well before mid-morning we had shed and tied them around our waists. Before us, we could see a broad, gently sloping hillside with no outstanding features. Enthusiasm for walking down that way was not high. Lower still was our zeal for having to make the walk back up. We began to discuss the planned events of the evening. Before dark we needed to set our rabbit snares and gather more firewood. So, Mr. Porter agreed that we should begin our return, but we should not go single file. If we spread out, we might see something that otherwise would be missed.

Not far from the spot to descend into the creek bottom I saw a bleached deer antler. It was a small Coes forked horn, or two-point antler. It must have been exposed to the sun for years, as it was chalk white and cracked, but I was happy to pick it up. It was the beginning of my new collection of horns and antlers.

We were the second scouting party to return to the camp. The group that had gone up the creek was still out, so the other two squads went about setting wire snares for cottontails. We had heard Gamble quail off and on, so I set some string snares for the birds, as well.

Some of us knew from experience that strangled rabbits or birds tasted about the same as critters that were taken any other way.

When the creek party showed up we were all anxious to hear what they had discovered. They'd seen several pools that held fish of different types. One kid had lugged back an old cow skull with nice horns. They reported a small snake that quickly slithered away into the water.

Upon finding some small fish Roy revealed the contents of his secret container. He had several freshly sharpened treble fishhooks and a small ball of fishing line. Roy and two others of the troop tied a sharp hook to a ten-foot piece of line and began snagging small fish. The largest of the fish was about six inches long and looked like trout, but one of the adults said they were Creek Chubs. The fishermen hoped to catch one fish for each scout, but only four fish were landed, to be added to the evening menu.

The scribes got at their work of composing the master map while the rest of us set more snares and gathered firewood. More small centipedes were announced, but no one gave them much attention. One kid was good with a slingshot and shot a large black lizard off of a tree. That reptile had blue and green markings on its neck. It did not look the least bit appetizing. Mr. Porter said that it should be gutted, skinned, and cooked, as good scouts did not kill just for fun. Some of the boys were squeamish, but I tried one of the overcooked tiny hind legs and thought it tasted like chicken or frog.

Supper was again primarily hot dogs with the tiny appetizer of roast lizard and overcooked fish. I shared my can of bleeped beans. As a special surprise, one of the adults produced two large packages of marsh mellows.

In the firelight, we sang songs and told stories of the day, as well as more old ghost stories before retiring. I had to mention Boris Karloff and the Wolfman. The man with the bugle blew "Taps" and we dutiful soldiers with feelings of jobs well done, crawled into our bags.

## Boys will be Boys - Matches and Flatulence

But the bugle was not to be the only source of music for the evening. The fat kid, Morris, was the first to open up. Flatulent emissions ranging in tone from piccolo squealers to tuba blasts punctured, and punctuated, the dark stillness of the night. We heard eruptions from adjacent tents as well as those from our shelter.

I've always appreciated nature's eloquent gift of natural gas, it's a form of methane, actually. In all but the most formal of occasions, flatulence brings forth spontaneous mirth and laughter, or at least a suppressed giggle. This evening was not a formal occasion.

Giggles and guffaws came from all quarters. Most of us were experiencing pubertal voice changes and tried to avoid higher pitched giggles, forcing our tones to lower octaves, but occasionally a girlish squeal would escape a scout's throat. Those lapses were never allowed to go without comment and derision from others in the vicinity. One of my close friends never made it through the voice change and carried that high squeaky voice into old age, the poor devil.

It was a veritable Frijole Philharmonic, though some of the musicians may have been a bit out of tune. A crescendo of natural sounds developed. A bandsman questioned if that should be called the "would wind" section or just the wind section. We pondered and debated that briefly.

Within any group of youngsters interested in achievement, a competition naturally developed. We were quick to discover and castigate those who attempted to substitute oral or underarm noises for the real thing.

There were buck snorts, barking spiders, girlish puffs, squealing Chickadees, bellowing bulls, groaning toads, and of course, silent vapors. There were machine gun bursts, bombs, ricochets, snaps, and screechers. What a splendid panoply of sounds were created by different sphincteral orifices! We tried to categorize and catalog the entire collection of noises. We wondered if .. and how, one could adjust his own emissions, to tune up his instrument, so to speak.

Andy, our scribe, took notes. This, no doubt, would be another of our contributions to man's understanding of the world around us.

We agreed that though the silent ones were less entertaining, they were also the most deadly, and had the clear advantage of stealth and surprise. A worthy feature in any battle.

But chunky Morris and his posterior had fallen mute. He, who had been so noisy in the morning was cursed with an uncompetitive silence after his initial blast that evening. I'm not sure anyone missed his contribution, however much we were expecting it. And he offered no explanation or apology for his lack of contribution. It was remarkably disappointing, to say the least.

One of our specially skilled troop members was producing convincing sounds by cupping his hand in his armpit and abruptly bringing his arm down. We asked that he desist that distracting disturbance. Such subterfuge was best reserved for school classrooms, or maybe, Sunday school.

Some deep-thinking fellow announced that he sure hoped that with all the straining, someone did not poop their pants.

Everyone it seemed, wanted to gain notoriety for producing the loudest, wildest, stinkiest emission, - something of truly noteworthy and memorable quality. Legends could be made here. Reputations could be earned.

At one point I thought I heard some adults talking. They, too, must have heard the music. I hoped they would not disperse the instrumentalists.

One of the more experienced older scouts in my tent, Eugene, the one who had dropped the loaf of bread, now, perhaps in an effort to redeem himself, announced that he believed abdominal vapors would burn. Others denied that it could happen.

Eugene offered to bet a quarter that he could burn his own vapors.

"Baloney", cried his detractors - actually they cried "bull excrement", but I attempt to eschew the use of crude terms.

The controversy took on the status of a serious debate.

Bets of twenty-five cents each were placed between several attendees, myself included. Knowing Eugene to be two years older than the rest in seventh grade, but generally competent, and much more experienced, I figured he surely knew the combustibility of such natural vapors was a certainty, or he wouldn't have risked a whole quarter. I bet my quarter on "yea".

Scouts from adjacent tents, having overheard the raging debate, crowded into our cramped shelter. All bets were covered and the great revelation was about to take place. Those not able to enter the tent crowded near the entrance, jostling to get at least their head inside the flap.

A few show-offs were expelling their gaseous ammunition, willy-nilly in their effort to gain fame and recognition. Our tent had become an aromatic cesspool. One scout gagged and crawled out.

We tried to keep the talking to a whisper, lest the adults discover our ignoble experiment and disperse the crowd before we had proof of flatulence combustibility one way or the other. It was literally a burning question.

One of our more cerebral scouts suggested that wasting potential scientific material was foolish and furthermore, so much gas in the tent could prove lethal if, in fact, the gas proved to be flammable. The whole tent might blow up or ignite! It would be tough to explain that to the doctors and our parents. Just think of the doctor or nurse asking, "Your lungs were singed by what?"

One kid said his eyes were burning from all the gas. My eyes were watering from all the laughter.

Another said that he heard his mother accuse his father of permeating the household upholstery with his flatulence, so he hoped his clothes would not permanently reveal his activities of that evening.

Another thinker wondered if smells would wash out in the laundry.

Could flatulents be as individually unique as fingerprints?

My observation was that smells were actually a form of matter and these smells that were entering our nostrils and were therefore traveling close to our brains, had just been expelled from someone's rear end. Furthermore, they had most likely been bubbling up for several feet or even yards, in close proximity to turds - the ultimate offal. My detailing of the origin of the abominable, abdominal vapors was met with some horrible expressions from my peers.

I made my attempt to make a valuable contribution to the discussion, but my offering was the most revolting and sobering consideration of all. However, some laughed, nonetheless.

So, at last, the moment of truth neared.

But Eugene had been coming up empty. Strain as he might, nothing came forth. He was under extreme stress and peer pressure for sure. His reputation and leadership status were at stake. After spilling the loaf of bread, he had some making up to do.

The nay-sayers began to demand their money back. Charges of outright fraud were voiced in disgust.

At last, Eugene, red in the face, eyes abulge, with the veins of his neck outstanding and his head in a high-frequency quiver, announced that he could feel one coming. All eyes were on his butt, upraised for all to easily view, near which he held a lighted match.

Those closest to Eugene edged back, just in case his forced emission had a lump in it or came with the force of a blowtorch. That was unnecessary as his underwear would surely retain any solids, but, nevertheless, they moved.

Our suspense and all doubts were extinguished when Eugene forced out a stupendous burst of natural vapor. It did not blow out the match, rather it "poofed", emitting a blue flame for all to witness.

After an initial stunned silence, unpremeditated whoops of amazement rent the night air. Even those that lost their wagers were joyous. Eugene was cheered as might befit a man of the order of Sir Isaac Newton, Benjamin Franklin, or Alexander Graham Bell.

I quickly pocketed my winnings as did the other winning people of faith.

Yep, there are so many things to be learned in life and scouting was such an instructive activity.

"Awright, you scouts, it's lights out and eyes shut, we have work to do tomorrow," came the announcement from Mr. Porter.

Of course, it took us some time to wind down after such an interesting and stimulating session, but eventually, things grew quiet, except for the occasional sound of the release of residual intestinal gases, accompanied by the inevitable giggles.

Some of us felt like we had become semi-scientists in the specialty field of flatulent philharmonics. Maybe a merit badge should be awarded for expertise in this field. I contemplated a design for such a badge - perhaps something resembling a mushroom cloud rising above a cesspool, or an outhouse.

## The morning after .. Sunday

The reveille was sounded before the first light. The adults made no mention of the previous night's activities, but we all knew they knew.

Oatmeal was the breakfast, wolfed down without complaint and we were ready to go as the first beams of sunlight broke over the cliffs to the east and began to spill down through the treetops of Arivaipa Canyon.

As to who would go where my squad and the other "mountain party" were both keen to travel the creek bottom. This was our last day, so Mr. Porter decreed that both would reconnoiter the riparian route.

Runners were dispatched to check their snares. One small cottontail rabbit and one large pack rat were proudly carried back for all to see. Due to the possibility of harboring the plague, the rat was buried. I, the only one in possession of experience in the art of skinning small game, got the honor of peeling and gutting the rabbit for later roasting. I put the cleaned carcass in an icebox.

We carried the master map, treated with reverence due to a biblical scroll, and protected in a paper towel tube. The merry band quickly pushed up the creek to the end of the previous day's trek. We were venturing into the unmapped, unknown beyond, intent on blazing a new trail. We thought of ourselves as modern-day Lewis and Clark explorers, the likes of Burton and Speke searching for the headwaters of the Nile, or maybe Mr. Stanley in his search for Dr. Livingston.

No big game had been reported by any of the three squads the day before, so we were excited to see a doe and fawn drinking from the creek ahead of us. They were Mule deer and quickly threw up their heads, ran for a short distance, then did their stiff four-legged "stotting"(or prancing) as they angled up the side hill. Their large ears, manner of running, and lack of a large white tail positively identified them as Mulies, which I was proud to announce to all.

We confirmed that several types of fish occupied the creek, as well as leopard frogs and a large host of ugly black water bugs.

I searched in vain for tadpoles.

Tracks of Javalina and fox were evident on the banks of the creek as were bird tracks of several types.

Mourning Doves were seen throughout the day. We sighted one Great Blue Heron.

High on the cliffs we identified what appeared to be caves, but we did not have time to approach or confirm them, much to the relief of the adults. I would have been happy to share my expertise in spelunking with the entire troop, as would Leon, but the opportunity was not to come.

Poor Andy was busy sketching our route and noting the things we saw. He faithfully performed his unenviable job, like a good Boy Scout. He seemed to enjoy his post.

The day was sunny and warm and the deep canyon had no wind, so most of us took a little swim - it was more like a wade or a sitz bath - in the creek, but the cool water felt good.

By mid-afternoon, once our three squads were reassembled at the bivouac site, the bugler blew the "assembly." He announced that we were to break camp and prepare to journey back to town. The cartographers were to update their maps as well as they could, then get together in town to produce three copies of the finished product Then the bugler blew the "recall " and we all fell to our work. We loved the bugle, as it brought to mind the old-time cavalry that not so many years ago had been active, perhaps in the very place we stood.

## FISHOOKS - TREBLE TROUBLE

Our great adventure to the "Every Viper" river had been extremely satisfying. Our only accident or injury was the slightly smashed finger of one of our group as we were riding in, and possibly sore ribs from laughing.

However on our last day, as we were getting ready to load our stuff into the trucks, Chunky Roy, who had enjoyed his fishing success, began sorting out his stuff. Not wanting anyone to be stuck by his treble fishhooks, he carefully placed them in a small box which he placed on the ground near a large stream-polished rock. Roy plunked his butt down in his usual fashion - when he stood over the place to sit he would slowly lower his rear end, then, when he sensed the grip of gravity, he would cease control of his descent and just plop down, as very young children are often seen to do.

But the slick rock he intended for his seat was not symmetrical and Roy slipped immediately to the ground - right onto his box of fish hooks.

Roy's piteous cry was heard by everyone. His considerable body weight combined with the few inches of descent was enough to crush the box of hooks and drive several of the sharpened nibs of the hooks through his britches and into the skin of his gluteal region.

The sharp treble hooks had been wonderful the day before as Roy snagged small fish from the water, but in today's situation, barbless hooks were clearly to be preferred.

Scoutmaster Porter and two more adults were soon at the scene. Amidst Roy's incessant howls of pain, the men told him to remain on the ground, as rising would only cause more pain. Roy would have to un- button his pants and roll onto his belly to allow clear access to his injured hind end. His pants had to be slit open to allow his healers to operate on the hooks.

Trouble comes in threes I had heard and three of the treble hooks had pierced Roy's body - two nibs from one hook and a single nib from the others. Luckily only one barb had buried itself in his now quivering flesh.

Mr. Porter and a school teacher used needle-nosed pliers to remove the first two nibs, but the barb required minor surgery. Someone came up with a razor blade and a slight incision was all it took to free the barb.

Throughout this field surgery, Roy's sphincter was silent - to the relief and amazement of us all.

A dousing of "Devils Spit" (merthiolate) and Roy was released.

After only thirty minutes we were loading the trucks and soon on the road.

Since I was probably the only one whose Mom regularly prepared rabbit, I was given the carcass to take home.

As we traveled I reflected on things I had gained on this trip. I had found one deer antler and an old mule shoe which I would present to the troop. I learned that beans produce music, whether heated or not. I had a more in-depth understanding of flatulence, its myriad forms, and the humorous benefits of that natural function. I wondered if colleges gave degrees in the subject. Maybe one could major or at least minor in that study.

And last, but far from least, I learned that flatulents were combustible - a bit of knowledge that might provide both money and entertainment for me and my friends in the future.

It had been a most enjoyable and productive camping trip.

Parents convened at Mr. Porter's house to pick up their kids and we headed home, full of satisfaction at our jobs well done and our heads full of new useful knowledge.

Friendships were made and strengthened. Knowledge was acquired. Maps were made. And laughs were had.

The deer antler and mule shoe I had found were added to the troop's collection of interesting artifacts. The kid who found the cow skull told us he planned to make powder horns, and would bring them to show when he finished crafting them.

However, the official highlight of the post-camping meeting was our map. The cartographers had drafted three identical copies and received top compliments from Mr. Porter. One of the copies had, in script so light it was discernible only under the closest scrutiny, a small "x" marking the location where Eugene had demonstrated his human torch stunt. It was, after all, a noteworthy event. The significance of that discrete mark was known only to us scouts. Who knows, a monument might someday in the future be erected there, to commemorate that momentous event.

Still chuckling over our flatulent philharmonic I checked the school library and found a copy of a small book by Benjamin Franklin, the title of which was "Fart Proudly". Well, if a brain so acclaimed as that of Ben Franklin could delve into the mysteries and fun of flatulence, how could we do less than give proper reverence to the subject? Forget the prudes and their correctness! Flatulence can be - and ought to be fun!

## Eugene - again and again

School, or jail as we referred to it, rocked along about as usual. Classrooms were severely overcrowded and not enough books were available for all the students, but we got by, and we had fun. Hardly anyone ever considered doing any homework. We spent time figuring out how to cheat by wiggling our ears, clearing our throats, coughing, etc.

After school, Monday through Thursday, we would practice baseball for two hours. As we got ready to take to the field everyone worked on their mitts, forming well-defined pockets that would help snag and retain any ball that came within reach. We all changed into our "play clothes," to avoid wear and tear on our good school duds.

On one never to be forgotten afternoon, Eugene was practicing with us. He was wearing an old pair of bib overalls that must have been his father's, as they were much too large for Eugene. When he ran, the body of the bibs billowed out like a balloon struggling to become airborne. That fateful afternoon, he rolled up the pant cuffs well above his ankles and enthusiastically worked his cleats into the dirt for a quick response to whatever came his way.

The coach picked up his Fungo bat and began to rapidly pop flies and grounders to fielders in left to right field.

A hot grounder came toward Eugene. As he charged toward its expected trajectory, he thrust his gloved left hand forward to scoop up the ball. But, somehow as his hand neared the ground, he stepped on the glove with his right foot. His sudden, twisted pile-up was spectacularly funny, far beyond my ability to describe.

Worst of all, at least for Eugene, his debacle was witnessed by the entire field of participants and onlookers.

Poor Eugene. Recalling his dumping the loaf of bread into the sand and other blunders, I began to wonder if the guy should be allowed to chew gum while walking or any other combination of activities of similar challenge and complexity.

By some sort of miracle, Eugene arose from the dust, brushed off his bibs, and assumed the crouched stance, indicating he was ready for another grounder. All eyes were upon him.

He successfully fielded several balls, then on his mad dash to get under a deep, high fly, the cleats of his left shoe pinned his fallen right pant cuff to the dirt and we were treated to another spectacular crash.

This time Eugene rose slowly. His cheek was scuffed and weeping specks of blood. The coach motioned for Eugene to come to the home plate. The wannabe fielder trotted forward with a noticeable limp, then dejectedly took his seat on the bench. A buddy helped pick bits of sand and gravel from his abraded face. His head was lowered - but not in reverence.

Eugene's bibs were faded and threadbare, showing several large holes. Surely they were cast-offs and not much to lose in any case. I asked him if maybe we should just cut off the overlong pant cuffs. He nodded in agreement. Every normal boy carried a picket knife in those days, so I pulled out my Barlow and cut both pant legs to mid-calf length. He kept the cut ends to give to his Mom for patching material. With his handicap removed, Eugene made the team, but provided less entertainment for the rest of us and the public audience throughout the rest of the baseball season.

But Eugene's notoriety had not yet reached its apex. One fine Saturday several of us schoolmates had bicycled up the road into the Catalina Mountain foothills. We were a group of five classmates that day, more numerous than usual for such adventures. Difficulties encountered in getting together such a large band of miscreants always made me prefer smaller groups or just going it alone. It's difficult to coordinate several nervous systems.

As I mentioned previously, Eugene was the oldest by two years and the largest by fifty pounds and two or three inches. There were old deserted dwellings of several types scattered about the foothills area which we planned to investigate. We parked our bikes at an old frame house with a set of corrals and the remains of a barn. The old homestead was in a pretty valley. Large scrub oaks were in abundance, it appeared to have once been the headquarters of an up-and-coming little ranch. A windmill, missing several blades, sat atop a galvanized metal tower. Between the corrals was a water trough made of local stream polished stones and concrete. Inside the trough was a residue of mossy water that had a lot of small black bugs skittering about its surface. We were glad to have packed along two canteens of tap water for each adventurer.

The general appearance of the house hinted that it had more amenities than most rural dwellings of its day. First, it was a frame house, not an adobe structure which was common to the area. Its corrugated tin roof was rusty, but in good condition, and the windows were all intact, which was most unusual for any deserted building.

I wondered why anyone would walk away from such an idyllic place.

We all set about exploring the house. We walked cautiously up the three steps to enter the covered porch with a hitching rail in front, taking great care to not break through the old warped planks. The weathered front door was ajar, so we pushed it open. The house had settled, causing the lower part of the door to drag against the plank floor. The sound that came forth was spooky and would have been unnerving if done in the dark. We were all primed to dash back outside if any hint of a malevolent life form issued from inside the building.

Of course, there were lots of spiderwebs throughout. Detritus, deposited by birds, rodents, the occasional fox, wind, and time, littered the floor. Our group of intrepid amateur investigators cautiously proceeded from the main room to the kitchen at the back of the house. We squeaked open the doors to the two bedrooms and to our surprise, found a small toilet in a tiny room off the hallway. The old porcelain commode was stained and unsightly but the stool as well as the water closet mounted above appeared to be in serviceable condition. The stool and water closet were both dry, as we imagined the bones of the former inhabitants must be.

One of our group spotted a framed area in the hallway ceiling. That had to be the access to the attic. We hopefully speculated that possibly firearms or other valuables might have been stored up there. We discussed who would be the one to check that out. No ladders were available so we decided to cup our hands together to make stirrups and boost one fellow up to see what might be lying in the high recess. We could thrash out how to divvy up the spoils if any were found. Thinking he might claim a gun or some other neat thing, Eugene wanted to be the guy to do the inspection, but he was too heavy, so he was elected to be one of the stirrup men. Jose, the smallest and most wiry of the group, got that prime assignment. I was the number two human hand stirrup.

Once Jose got hoisted high enough, he dislodged the lid covering the hole and gingerly stuck his head into the attic space. As we hefted Jose higher so that he might leverage himself fully into the attic, he let out a howl and dropped back. We all scurried away from the opening, expecting a vampire or werewolf to come flying out. Once down with both feet securely on the floor, Jose caught his breath and told us that something touched the back of his neck.

None of our group had brought a flashlight on that trip, so we debated what it could have been that had buggered Jose. Who would be the next to check the cavernous attic was our next decision.

Eugene, secure in the knowledge that we could not lift his biomass, heartily professed his courage and said that he longed to be the next to go up.

Finally, we settled on Jack as the next to go. Jack, the next strongest in the group and normally a boisterous type, was circumspect in his approach to the dark attic. Before he had stuck his head above the rim of the access hole he announced that he could see a small cord hanging down and that must be what had caressed Jose's neck and spooked him.

Just to sweeten the apprehension, I wondered aloud if the cord was a hangman's noose ready to apply to whomever next stuck his head in there.

Jack dropped down and gave me a dirty look.

After some procrastination, we again convinced Jack of the necessity of investigating that mysterious space and we thrust his body up. The endeavor took on the character of entering an overhead catacomb. He gripped the edges of the hole and eased himself higher into the dark space. With Eugene and me pushing on the soles of his boots, Jack got firmly situated inside the gloomy attic. He said he had to sit still and let his eyes get accustomed to the dim light. In a minute or so, he said there was nothing up there but rat turds and dust. Not wanting to linger longer, he let himself down and dusted off his pants.

I thought this site had the makings of a perfect place to bring some girls on Halloween night. I could well imagine the screams of horror we could elicit from some of the young damsels as well as some of the less-than-stalwart young fellows in our class. I envisioned pretty girls jumping into my arms and hugging me in confusion, terror ... and gratitude.

We shook the abundant rodent droppings off before leafing through some weathered old magazines and Sears Roebuck catalogs. We pried open and scrutinized old tobacco tins, finding only dust and stale air. The cigarette paper sleeves were empty. We finally became convinced that there was nothing salvageable left inside, so we focused on the surrounding yard area.

One of the group announced that he had found a square nail, but it was only from a horseshoe, nothing unique. Nevertheless, he pocketed his find.

Eugene had proceeded to the backyard area kicking over loose boards and rocks, bent on making a noteworthy discovery when suddenly he let out a whoop.

It was a serious cry of anguish.

A snake or tarantula came to mind as I rushed to see what had bitten Eugene. When I rounded the corner of the house, Eugene was yelling bloody murder, but I could only see his head and shoulders. He had fallen into a hole.

Slowing my advance to a more cautious pace and watching where I placed each foot, in my attempt to avoid a similar fate, I was struck by the all too familiar smell of human sewage. Eugene had broken through the rotten, half-buried wooden cover of an old cesspool!

Oh, yeah, that a toilet normally had a cesspool or septic tank on the other end, occurred to me, but the revelation came too late.

Eugene was swearing using terms, some of which I had never heard before. It occurred to me that our eardrums might be in danger of being blistered by his cursing. As he thrashed about trying to free himself from the horrendous muck - it was quite literally awful .... or offal, one might say, and in his struggle, he was slopping the stinking juice and semi-solid globs of you-know-what around.

I held back, as did the other three adventurers who stood in dumbfounded silence.

Eugene was pleading for someone to help him get out, but nobody wanted to touch him. To grip his hand would transfer his new coating to whoever attempted to offer assistance to our fallen comrade. To approach too closely might result in actually joining Eugene in his private bathing pool. Our friendship was strong, but common sense prevailed, at least for the moment.

This was akin to being up poop creek without a paddle, or even worse, I suppose.

Eugene's hollering and his staccato stream of epithets kept us all on edge. Our minds were temporarily overloaded and befuddled. We were mind-boggled.

After what I'm sure must have seemed like half of forever to Eugene, I told our floundering friend that I would go find a board or something to assist in extracting himself from that disgusting mire.

"Remain calm, Eugene," was my sage advice.

"Calm, how could anyone be calm while he's alone inside a cesspool?" was Eugene's sputtering reply.

One of the top rails of the corral was loose, enabling me to pry it free, and then I rushed with it to Eugene's rescue. As I engaged in this I wondered if the contents of cesspools might ferment over a long period of time.

I told the others to help me on my end of the pole. With Eugene firmly gripping the other end, we slowly drug his stinking, thrashing body free. He slimed his way out, then stood up and fully realizing his condition, he began to sob. I felt terrible that he was losing his composure in this manner, especially in front of so many witnesses.

The rest of us backed off, keeping well clear of our cursed companion.

I wanted to help my friend, but I didn't want to share in his misery. Then I had a thought.

"Hey, Eugene, if your clothes were on fire, what would you do?" I asked.

Afflicted as he was with the humiliation, as well as the stench of his situation, he offered no response, other than to give me a dirty look.

"Eugene, you would roll in the sand to snuff out the flames, right? So lie down in the sand wash and then shake and brush off the stuff. It can't hurt, can it? It isn't called a sand wash for nothing." I suggested.

I heard some snickering coming from Jack and the others, so I shot them a disapproving glare.

"Now, do it quick before that stuff dries on you, Eugene," I urged.

My bedeviled buddy lowered his head, stopped the sobbing, and dejectedly shuffled toward the sand wash. I followed along behind at a safe distance, out of arm's reach, for sure.

Eugene got to the dry wash and started to remove his Levi jacket,

"No, no, Eugene, do it with your clothes on to get that crap off your duds," I told him.

So that's what he did. A rusty old shovel was in the corral, so I used it to heap sand on him as he rolled around. The others tossed handfuls of sand to assist as best they could. As he attempted to brush himself off, I checked again at the water trough, but that green, slimy liquid offered no hope of improvement for Eugene. There would be no water rinse for our buddy until he got home.

We spent a good half hour trying to decontaminate our companion, but his fragrance remained easily identifiable. We realized that it was what it was and we all would have to endure it for however long it might take - but from a considered distance.

Anyone who knew us would consider us to be close friends, but no one wanted to be any closer to Eugene than absolutely necessary that day.

We didn't even want to be downwind of our buddy.

The group consensus was that we should all head home.

Several pick-ups slowed down as they passed us on the road home. Two offered a ride, but to spare Eugene further mortification, we did not mention why we were returning with so much daylight left. We just thanked them for the kind offer and peddled on.

Feeling somehow, at least partially responsible for Eugene's plight, Jose and I accompanied our still-wet and reeking buddy to his house.

His clothes were only damp by the time we got to town, but he was still producing an easily identifiable, nauseating miasma. His entire body was enclosed in a Devil's halo of smell. Jose and I waited in the front yard as Eugene entered the door. In milliseconds, Eugene was right back outside with his mother hollering at him. She told him to go to the backyard and strip off his clothes. Once that was done, she uncoiled the garden hose and sprayed him off thoroughly as he stood naked and shivering, clutching his crotch with both hands. Then she asked if we needed a hosing, too. We politely declined her kind offer.

Her boy was the only one so afflicted, but we did not mention that to his mother. I suspect that his mother had been through similar scenarios with Eugene, as he was truly unique in so many unattractive ways.

In thinking about Eugene's accident ... more of an incident, really .. well ... it was an experience for sure, it could have happened to any of us. Or was it his larger size and extra fifty pounds that did it? I decided that it was mainly just his pure bad luck that led to his baptismal emersion in the sewer juice. Poor guy, I truly felt sorry for him.

Monday morning came as it inevitably does and Eugene was in school, but he was more subdued than normal. His ego bruised, he seemed to semi-submerge socially and did not join our gang on any weekend exploratory trips for some time.

## The Door Knob

Some weeks later as the noon bell rang, Leon was the first to the door. He flung the door wide open and took off for the lunch room, with his long hair blowing in his own, self-generated breeze. Unfortunately, Eugene was running from another classroom, full tilt, down the covered outside walkway. His head was down and he was churning along in a sprinter's stance. Eugene looked up just in time to meet the doorknob Leon had flung open connect with his right eye. Leon heard the impact, too, but after a quick glance back, resumed his own dash speed, and was quickly around the corner, and out of sight.

Warmed-over fried chicken was on the menu.

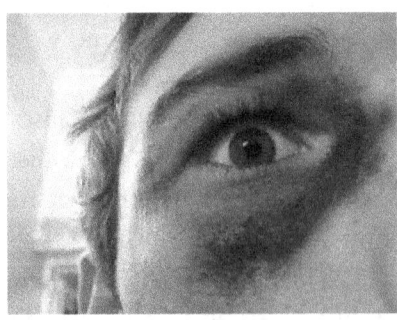

Eugene wore his black eye for a long time.

The large, heavy solid core door just vibrated from the force of the impact with Eugene's peri-orbital bones.

Immediately after Eugene's eyebrow connected with the door, he was laid out flat on his back and unconscious.

Several of us stopped to help Eugene, who soon shook his head, got to his feet, and charged on toward the feed of chicken. He displayed a multicolored black eye for more than a week. It would have killed most guys, but it did not interfere with his appetite - or his eternally bad luck.

## The weekend party

Some people just seem to have nothing but bad luck. Eugene was one of those unfortunate few.

Months later, at one of our senior high school parties, we convened a large group at an old mine site. There were more than a dozen vehicles, full of high school juniors and seniors, with a few recent graduates as well.

The abandoned plant we selected for the evening activities had one large platform that sat elevated about five feet above ground level. The main room had a flat concrete floor that was just right for dancing. There was no need to take our shoes off to dance here, unlike at the "sock hops" held at the school basketball court on its pampered hardwood floor. Besides, we suspected multitudes of scorpions, centipedes, and tarantulas were lurking in the old structure and we wanted to avoid barefooted confrontations with any form of arachnid.

By propping up some old corrugated roofing we could reflect the car or pick-up headlights onto the dance floor which produced an eerie effect. It was perfect for our needs.

Someone had a battery-powered record player (this was an age before the invention of boom boxes) and we were jitterbugging, slow dancing, and swinging away. We could make all the noise we wanted in this isolated place without complaints or intervention by anyone to quiet us down. And cleanup would be our option. It was truly a perfect site for our grand ball.

We had several cases of soda pop, tons of cookies, popcorn balls, Fritos, and other light-snacking treats.

As is inevitable with a group that large, and of that age, - except at Mormon parties - somebody brought some booze. There were a couple of cases of beer and maybe a bottle or two of hard liquor that turned up and was made available to all. I was using Dad's '55 Chevy pick-up and did not imbibe even a taste, but many of the participants took a snort or two, Eugene included. By then, Eugene was twenty-one years old and could legally drink, so apparently, he indulged in more than a couple of snorts.

Everybody, even the worst troublemakers, was behaving. Nobody wanted to spoil the fun.

With all the physical activity and the volume of soda pop being consumed, naturally, people would need bladder relief. A high wall at the back of the platform had a door in the middle that led to a loading ramp. The guys were going out to the loading ramp where they stood to pee off the edge. The girls were discretely taking care of their bladder relief necessities out of sight and behind another building.

Eugene, with his extra years of practice, was one of the best dancers in school and had been "cutting a rug", as they say, on the concrete all evening. He'd been dancing with most of the girls and getting lots of ladies' choice requests, some even while dancing with another girl. It was clearly a great night for Eugene. I was happy for him.

But, I had observed him taking surreptitious sips from a waxed cup that he kept stashed high enough on a beam that others could not reach. I figured it probably was booze and I hoped that he would not overdo it. I also figured Eugene had not much practice in drinking hard liquor.

Suddenly, amidst all this fun, I realized that Eugene had not been on the floor for some time. I doubted that he would walk away from all the attention he was getting, so I asked around. No one had seen him for quite some time. I wondered. I checked and saw that his Dad's pick-up was parked where he left it when we set up the reflecting sheets of metal. He had to be nearby. Not to worry, I figured.

But I kept dancing and jostling around with friends.

After about a half hour or so, I heard nature's call and walked out the door to the ramp to relieve myself. While in midstream I heard a moan from below the ramp. When I peered over the edge, there was Eugene, lying face-up, soaked by me and who knows how many others.

Oh my gosh, I redirected my stream, zipped up, ran to the edge, jumped off the ramp, and went to Eugene. Oh, was he ever wet! I yelled at him to get up. He reached for my hand, but as on that sewage-contaminated time just a few weeks before, I didn't want to touch my buddy due to the state in which I found him.

My hollers brought several more fellows to the ramp. They quickly joined me at Eugene's side.

What a crying shame! This guy, king of the dance floor, was reduced to Colonel of the Urinal, or some such ignoble position.

One of the newly arrived witnesses began to laugh and I told him to shut up, as we needed to help Eugene, not just make fun of him. After all, he was a good egg, and I did like the guy.

John Barleycorn had so addled Eugene's brain that he was not aware of his ignominious situation. He was babbling something about how he was going to try a backflip with his next dancing partner. He got to his feet, but wobbled around and fell back onto that oft-anointed, and specially muddied ground. He mumbled that he didn't know how he had gotten so sweaty. It wasn't sweat.

In all my eighteen years I had never seen anyone so inebriated. It can creep up on a guy, especially when he's inexperienced and having so much fun, I guess.

That sort of put a damper (no pun intended) on Eugene's evening of dancing. He managed to get on his feet once again and asked me what happened.

Assuring him that everything would be all right, I asked if anyone had a spare jacket or a ground cloth. Most people carried a piece of cloth or rug in their vehicle to place on the ground for changing a tire or other auto work, which was commonly necessary. Kids took care of their good clothes, as well as their vehicles, in those days. One of the guys said he would go get his chunk of rug.

I told Eugene to brace himself on the edge of the ramp until we could help him. In his confused state, he just looked at me, bleary-eyed. He had always trusted me and I was careful to not betray his trust.

Shortly the kid with the ground cloth appeared. I draped it over my right forearm, and told Eugene to hold my arm, as I escorted him to his pickup. Eugene left a trail of drips that drained from his clothes, as he shuffled along with me. The group that had been drawn to the scene formed a tight knot as we walked back toward the parked vehicles. I elicited promises from each to never mention Eugene's shameful situation ... to anyone, ever. What had befallen my friend was only partially his fault. We needed to cover for him. We had already covered him with urine.

I asked Eugene for his keys, which he dug out of his pocket and handed to me. I told him that he was really drunk and would have to sleep it off in the bed of the truck. When the party was over, either I or someone else would drive him back to town. Eugene curled up in the fetal position and soon was asleep. Actually, he just completely passed out.

With our friend put to bed, so to speak, we all went back to the party, but we took turns checking on our buddy until the party ended a couple of hours later.

One of the non-drinkers did not have a vehicle and was a responsible kid, so he was assigned to drive Eugene's Dad's truck home. I followed until our sodden friend's truck was properly parked and he was escorted inside his house. I suggested that he best quietly peel off his clothes, take a shower, and go to bed. It was in the wee hours, well past three o'clock in the morning. I assume that Eugene's Mom was sound asleep and after a few minutes of no sounds, I figured my friend had done as I had suggested, so I drove home.

After graduation, we all scattered to the far corners of the world. I went back to Montana, several joined the Navy, and Eugene joined the Marines.

I never heard of Eugene again. His last name was French and a bit comical sounding, but I will not divulge it here, as he may still be alive somewhere and, through thick and thin, he was my buddy. I miss him.

## Cutting our own hair

When the cost of a haircut went to two dollars and fifty cents, Pop told me that was ridiculous. He bought a set of electric hair clippers in Tucson for about seven dollars and we cut each other's hair from then on.

Hairstyles have changed a lot since the 1950s. Most guys my age had crew cuts or butch cuts, not only were they "in style," but they could easily be self-done at home. A few, - those with limited imagination, or bitten by conformity, - wore the traditional college or executive cut, parted on one side and combed to the other side. I had a flattop, which I could do myself at home. Later I grew out the sides and wore what was called a "flattop with fenders." After Elvis gained popularity, his style of mop became the rage, but I didn't like long hair ... or Elvis.

Butch wax scented stick wax (all varients of Hair Jam), Vaseline Hair Tonic, and Vitalis were popular with many, but I saved my money and used only water. Some fifty years later I was informed that Vitalis did not have the magic that Viagra did.

While on the ranch in Montana, I wore a hat most of the time and my hair did whatever the hat and my sweat dictated.

No guy would be caught dead wearing an earring. Tattoos were seen on a few kids' hands and arms - they were usually home-done and were considered cheap and tacky - very low class.

## SNEAKING IN

The little desert town of San Manuel had no regular movie theater, but it had a drive-in. The projection building had a small area with about two dozen reasonably comfortable seats for those who wished to use them. Before anyone in my age bracket could drive, we would peddle our bicycles the mile or so to the drive-in, pay the admission price, park the bikes near the building, and enjoy the film. I don't recall anyone having any sort of lock for their bicycle.

It wasn't long before one of our group found (or made) a hole in the fence at the far back side of the lot. The news of this secret portal was guarded but spread quickly, nevertheless. The wires had been snipped to make a hole big enough to allow even a girl in a billowy dress to crawl through. Once the passage had been made, the swinging "door" in the chain link fence was carefully replaced to make detection by the drive-in maintenance man challenging. We used this reduced-price entrance unnoticed by the operators as well as the paying customers for several months before a group of kids was caught and taken to the police station. Worst of all, their names were published in the local newspaper, The San Manuel Miner. That ended our free movies, as no one wanted to be apprehended, labeled a cheat, and have the community-wide notoriety that would follow being named in the paper. All good things must come to an end it seems. So many petty crimes are fine, as long as their perpetrators are not exposed.

## CHAUFFEUR

When finally I turned eighteen in March of my senior year, I took the test and became a licensed chauffeur. My interest was not in driving some overly self-important rich dude or dame around, but in driving trucks, as I had done at the ranch in Montana. I had been getting some part-time work at the local furniture store and my chauffeur's license soon led me to be hired to drive the delivery truck. By hiring me the big-headed store owner would not have to demean himself with such an undignified, menial chore.

The new secretary/bookkeeper at the store was in her mid-twenties and very attractive. She was friendly with everyone, including me and the two part-time employees who helped deliver furniture. One of the other boys said she seemed to really "like" us. Personable employees, especially pretty women are an asset to any business, I figured.

The owner seemed to have an abiding interest in his secretary/bookkeeper and would have more time to "go over the books" with her if I picked up the furniture from the wholesalers as well as drove for the town deliveries. Soon I was taking the big panel truck to Tucson and Phoenix on Saturdays to get new stock for the store. Late one Saturday afternoon I brought in the truck full of new stuff, including new beds, box springs, and mattresses. I picked up a kid to help me unload the stuff, backed in toward the loading door behind the store and we off-loaded the large pieces. I closed up, parked the truck, hung the keys on their hook in the office, and went home.

Right after supper, I was ready to borrow my Dad's pick-up to take my date to the high school "kid dance" and realized that I must have left the keys to his pick-up with those for the furniture store truck.

There was only one thing to do. I walked back to the store, used my key to open the back door, and headed for the office to get my personal key ring.

Upon opening the office door I visually flashed on clothes laid upon the desk, then I saw there, on the office floor, was a new, top quality, queen-size mattress upon which were the owner and the bookkeeper. They were clothes-free and going at it.

Surely any responsible retailer should test his wares before foisting them on his customers, I guess.

The woman shrieked and the owner got up cussing angrily. I told him I needed my truck keys. Still cussing, he threw a whole cluster of keys at me, which I caught and backed out the door. Both lovers were still making a lot of uncomfortable noises when I exited the back of the store.

I figured that come Monday, I would no longer be driving for that furniture company.

After school on Monday, I stopped by the store on schedule to see if any local deliveries were to be made. I was braced for an uncomfortable scene with the owner. Expecting him to be somewhat restrained in the presence of customers, I walked in the front door. Several customers were admiring the new stuff in the display room, assisted by the secretary. I went directly to the office. No one was there and the new mattress was no longer on the floor. Well, I figured it must have proved worthy of selling to trusting buyers.

As I turned toward the display room, the secretary met me with a big smile and told me that she had some addresses for me to deliver furniture to and that the keys were hanging on a nail near the back door. When I was finished, she said I should use that place for the keys in the future. She handed me several receipt papers and, with a genuine full-body hug, she thanked me! I became aware of her considerable pectoral prominences.

Well, I never would have dreamed that things would go that well. I continued to drive for the store for nearly three months, until time to go back to Montana. No mention was ever made of my "Saturday night surprise" and the secretary retained her position .... of employment, I mean, for several years. Product testers are not easy to come by, I reckon.

In fact, the store began to advertise "Saturday Surprise" sales. I felt partially responsible for their advertising strategy and got a kick out of that.

## The Packard

Leon's Dad's Packard

One of my classmates, Leon, was a year or two older than the rest of us. His Dad had a 1953 Packard with automatic transmission and often loaned it to Leon for dates. We were sophomores in high school and full of energy - with a good dose of harmless deviltry thrown in.

Leon liked to drive fast and was pretty experienced and thought himself skillful at high-speed automobile manipulation. He, another classmate, Dick, and I were all in the Packard with our dates one evening when Leon steered us down the river road. Parallel to the San Pedro River ran another road that coursed over some roller coaster hills. At high speed when we topped out, those in the back seat would come clear off the cushions and sometimes hit their heads on the top of the interior. We had the same sensation in our bellies as one gets on some carnival rides. It was great fun.

That particular evening Leon had consumed a couple of beers, all by himself, as Dick and I abstained from drinking on dates and most any other time. We made the run through the roller coaster hills to the north, then turned around to head back south for a sequel to that thrilling episode.

One of the dips had an abrupt ditch in it, a product of a recent gully-washer rain. (Some locals called such rain storms "turd floaters".) We called it the doomsday wash. I thought it was the third one from the north end. As we roared back along the road I reminded Leon that the next one was the bad one. He insisted that we still had one good wash to go and floor-boarded the Packard up the hill. We topped out, felt the exhilarating belly tickle and I hollered again, that the ditch was coming up fast. Just past halfway down the hill, Leon realized that this, indeed, was the doomsday wash. He slammed on the brakes, the Packard crabbed sideways, Leon straightened it out and we hit the ditch going way too fast and came to a dead stop.

Cars didn't come with seat belts back in those days and Dick's date, I'll call her Stella, was propelled from the back seat forward until her nose stopped just short of smacking into the dashboard. Her feet hit the ceiling and when she came down, my head was under her dress and in between her bare thighs.

Poor Stella was thrust into the front seat on her belly with her bare legs coming down on my shoulders in the back seat. We were enveloped in a shroud of choking dust. I was also enveloped in a shroud of a pleated skirt and bare legs. And the engine had quit. Stella's Toni Permanent Wave was disheveled, but her attention was on the location of my head.

"Jake, it WAS this wash with the ditch," Leon admitted.

Dick's date struggled to get her upper body into the back seat where her legs were. As she squealed, squirmed, and struggled to belly-worm her way over the back of the front seat, she realized that my head was not in an area with which she was comfortable and she yelled to me to get my head out from between her legs.

Half blinded by her pleated skirt and who knows what else (one's imagination is appropriate here), I started laughing and tried to assist her by lifting one of her legs to place it with the other, but this caused her to screech and clamp them together. It was her involuntary response to a perceived threat to her nether region, I suppose.

I laughed even harder. My date, Denise (I suppose she was somebody's niece), was yanking on my arm to extract me from my position as she hollered, "Jake, get your head out from under her skirt!"

As Stella agitated her way back, her legs pinned my ears backward and it felt like they were going to get sheared right off. She twisted around until she was belly up and I pulled her into the back seat.

One could hardly be expected to keep their eyes clamped tightly shut given an opportunity... I mean ... situation like this - a truly unforeseeable scenario.

Miraculously no one was hurt ... and I didn't get slapped.

But, still laughing, I had to ask Stella if she had been planning on going to a polka dance, with those pok-a-dot panties on. She reeled back to slap me, but my good friend Dick, laughing as hard as I was, stayed her hand.

The laughter abruptly stopped as the gravity of our situation dawned on us all.

It took several attempts, but Leon got the engine running. When he tried to move the automatic shift lever, it was stuck. After some pushing and pulling it went into reverse gear, but regardless of what the gear indicator showed, the Packard would only go forward.

'We all got out and began to kick down the steep sides of the ditch. After several attempts, we got the car across the gully and headed for home at a top speed of twenty miles per hour with the gear still indicating reverse.

We were all dusty and dry-mouthed. Luckily, Leon's date had some Black Jack chewing gum which she shared with the group. The hour was late when we got to town, still creeping along at a slow speed.

As we came to the paved road, a Police car turned on its flashing lights.

"We were going so slow, the cop would naturally suspect we were drinking. (Of course, Leon had been drinking.) Quick, spit out your gum,"

Leon commanded. The girls all surrendered their gum and gave it to Leon, to use in the hope that his breath would not reveal that he had those two beers. Leon gobbled up the ABC (already been chewed) gum, spoke courteously with the policeman, and we were allowed to go on home.

Needless to mention, Leon no longer was allowed to use his Dad's Packard. I recall that after a few weeks, it was back in use, but only by his parents.

## A Saturday drive

But time heals all, so the saying goes. People have a short memory as well and later that year Leon's older brother Jack was allowed to take the other family vehicle, an older pick-up truck for a Saturday spin. He dutifully gathered up his buddies, including me, and we headed off down to the San Pedro River, east of town. I was one of the three who got to ride in the front seat, along with Jack, who was driving, and Leon. Four more of our male friends were in the back. It was an exceptionally hot, dusty ride along the dirt and sand road of the river bottom. The guys in the back put handkerchiefs over their faces to combat the suffocating dust. I reminded the outside riders that dust was nothing but mud with the juice squeezed out. They didn't think it was all that funny.

Jack's Dad's pickup when we started.

Jack planned to go to the site of Redington, then up the road toward Mount Lemmon in the Catalina Mountains.

Redington was officially a ghost town that had sprung up in 1875. As the story went, brothers Henry and Lem Redfield founded the little town and wanted a post office named for them, but the United States Postal Service said they could not use the name of a living person on a government post office, so the brothers chose the name, Redington. They got the post office in 1879 and Henry was the postmaster, but in 1883 Lem was lynched in Florence for robbing a stagecoach not far from that tiny desert town, which, by the way was the location of the Territorial Prison. We kids knew some of the ranchers in the area and thought maybe they could put us on some interesting sites for our investigations in that area, but they seemed to want to discourage our inquiries.

When we arrived at the spot that should be Redington we were at the head of a cloud of dust that stretched back up the road for as far as we could see. We found no one around, and even the abandoned buildings were reduced to next to nothing, so Jack headed up the first semblance of a road we came upon. We had already swallowed most of our canteens of water and hoped for a clean trough or someplace to water up, but we found only withered creosote brush, dust, and desiccated desolation.

When we came to an old double-walled adobe house with a shed roof on one side, Jack decided it would be fun to use the truck to try to bulldoze down one of the shed's side walls which had only a single course of adobe bricks.

Kids get some weird ideas of what would be fun, and some never graduate from such ridiculous inspirations. I've noticed that too often, the kids that never seem to grow up, become politicians.

I told Jack that if it was me, I wouldn't do any damage to the old structure, as the building, dilapidated or not, could maybe be put to some use, by whoever owned it - or someone.

Jack said it was falling down anyway and probably nobody owned or wanted it, so why shouldn't we have some fun knocking it down?

I told him again that I wouldn't be doing that, but if he was bound and determined to knock down the wall, I asked him to wait until I could find a good jar to put scorpions in, as I was sure we would find plenty of the nasty natured little stinger-tailed bugs when the old deteriorated mud bricks began coming apart.

We easily found the house's garbage dump. All the old places had one nearby in those days. I recovered a cracked, but still intact quart Mason jar, but couldn't find a lid to fit it. Oh well, I figured the sides of the jar were high enough to hold the bugs until we could find a cover for the top. I picked up a rusty old pair of pliers to use for catching the scorpions. I worked the pliers back and forth and pulled the truck's dipstick for some oil to overcome the rust and make them functional. When I was ready, I told Jack to go easy on the bulldozing, so I could grab as many bugs as possible before they found new places to hide. My eighth-grade teacher, Mr. Don McClure, and I had been selling all kinds of live wild critters from scorpions to rattlesnakes to a buyer in Tucson. Scorpions brought ten cents each. Three of those nasty bugs would buy us a gallon of gasoline!

Jack eased up to the wall and began to push with the front bumper of the truck. The adobe bricks began to crack apart and sure enough, scorpions began to come out, all of 'em mad as hops. I got three in my jar before the whole wall came down. A cloud of dust with a plume like a nuclear explosion ensued and everyone stepped away. It happened too sudden and I only got one more scorpion before they were all out of sight. Some of the scurrying insects actually left little plumes of dust behind them. The other kids wanted nothing to do with the venomous bugs, even at ten cents apiece. They stayed well away from the collapsed wall. I kept a nervous eye on where I put my feet.

Fired up by his success with the shed wall, Jack lined up and began pushing on an interior wall that was double thick. His back wheels began to spin and instead of the wall coming down, we heard a metallic crack and saw that his front bumper had busted where it attached to the frame, allowing one side to droop down a good six inches.

Jack got extremely angry and started cussing up a storm. Leon said that their Dad was going to be super torqued when he saw a second vehicle messed up so soon after the Packard. Jack backed the truck away from the building and assessed the damage. One side of the bumper was completely loose and the other was hanging on a cracked steel brace. We could try to wire up the broken side or just finish busting the other side off. Jack said we couldn't trust the rusty baling wire we found to hold the broken end, so we should just pry the other end loose and put the whole bumper in the back of the truck. After a lot of pushing and prying, that is what we did. Jack said he would think of some way to get the bumper back in place so his Dad wouldn't realize what had happened to the truck. I figured there was little to no chance of him doing that.

No, I wouldn't have done that with my Dad's truck .. or anyone else's.

As Jack put the truck in reverse, I noticed I was holding the mason jar with the scorpions at a bit of a slant and one of the stinger-tailed bugs was about to reach the rim, so I uprighted it and then set it down under a mesquite tree. I remembered to pick it up as we departed and nestled it between the spare tire and a toolbox in the back. The bugs were pretty agitated and were beginning to fight each other. I told the guy riding in the back to keep an eye on my jar of valuable bugs.

Bumperless or not, Jack was not to be distracted from his ultimate goal. After the delays at the old adobe structure, we were behind schedule, so Jack decided to head south and down the river instead of west toward the Catalina Mountains. A freak spring flash flood the week before had the road in pretty bad condition. We came to a badly eroded wash, where Jack forged ahead, only to become thoroughly stuck in the sand and mud just a few yards shy of the opposite bank. Rats!

Not long into our efforts to move the truck, as we lined up to push, I happened to look over the tailgate and noticed that the bug jar was tipped over, just as Henry yelled that he saw a scorpion coming out from a crack in the pick-up bed. Everybody jumped back from the truck. The sudden disengagement from pushing was unknown to Jack and he stepped down on the gas pedal and dug the rear tires deeper into the sand - all the way to the axel.

This development meant that someone had to get down in the muddy mess to scoop muck out from in front of the rear tires. As the scorpion capture was my idea, and therefore their escape was my responsibility, I was unanimously elected to do the job. I simply had no defense, so I set about getting the chore done. I emerged soaked and filthy, which exiled me to the back of the truck for the rest of the trip. I decided that thirty cents worth of bugs just wasn't worth it. And then the doggone scorpions all got away, anyway. Drats!

We cut brush and broke small branches off to place under the rear tires, but even with all of us but Jack pushing, as we nervously kept an eye out for escaped scorpions, it took over an hour to get unstuck and up the opposite bank. Four-wheel drive would have been nice.

We sure didn't want to go back through that muck hole, so Jack figured we'd best head to the town of Benson. Our day trip was going to be much longer than we'd planned.

When we got to Benson, the fuel gauge was bouncing on empty, so we all dug into the depths of our pockets and pooled our meager cash. Surprisingly enough, our gang of eight boys had a grand total of seven dollars and sixty-eight cents. Gas at the station in Benson was twenty-nine cents a gallon, so we pumped three gallons of gas, filled our water canteens for free from a hose, and went on to Tucson. We pumped another ten gallons in Tucson where the price was twenty-five cents a gallon. Our small mob of piebiters was on the verge of starvation, so we stopped at a grocery store and bought a couple of loaves of bread, a small jug of catsup, and two packs of hot dogs. We still had a little change left over for emergencies, but not enough for Pepsi cola, candy bars, or milkshakes all around, so the water would have to do.

Jack said his mother had told him to be in with the pick-up before dark and now we were in a race against darkness. We four grunts in the back were wind-blown and deeply sunburned long before we got home. It was well past sunset when we got through Tucson. When we approached Jack's driveway, he figured he'd get a tongue lashing from his Dad, so he dropped us off a block from his place and told us all to find our own way home.

Considering all, Jack decided it prudent to just fess up about the bumper coming off, but not belabor his confession with details. His story was that the durned thing came loose after a few miles on the bumpy corduroy river road and after careful inspection, we all decided it best to remove it for reinstallation back in town. His Dad thought that was good judgment. After school for several evenings, I went to help with the job and decided that welding was a skill I needed to acquire.

So, to the surprise of many, our little gang of rapscallions all graduated from high school in late May, 1960. Leon joined the Navy, his brother Jack went to work in the mine, our buddy, Eugene signed up with the United States Marines and was never heard from again, and me, I boarded a DC3 which flew me back to Montana and the Staunton Ranch, for my hoped for, but never realized, future as a cowboy.

www.ingramcontent.com/pod-product-compliance
Lightning Source LLC
Chambersburg PA
CBHW071840230426
43671CB00012B/2023